WRITEPLACER SUCCESS ADVANTAGE+ EDITION: ACCUPLACER ESSAY WRITING STUDY GUIDE

Note: Accuplacer and Writeplacer are registered trademarks of the College Board, which is neither affiliated with nor endorses this publication.

Writeplacer Success Advantage Plus Edition: Accuplacer Essay Writing Study Guide

Copyright © 2013. Academic Success Media. © Copyright 2020. Academic Success Group.

All rights reserved. No part of this publication may be reproduced, stored in a retrieval system, or transmitted, in any form or by any means, electronic, mechanical, photocopying, recording, or otherwise.

ISBN: 978-1-949282-54-2

COPYRIGHT NOTICE: Educators and other users are not permitted to copy these materials for distribution to or use by students. A copy of this publication should be purchased for each student.

Note: Accuplacer and Writeplacer are registered trademarks of the College Board, which is neither affiliated with nor endorses this publication.

TABLE OF CONTENTS

Writeplacer Essay Format & Question Types	1
Writeplacer Scoring – How the Automated Scoring Software Works	3
How to Avoid Common Writeplacer Errors and Raise Your Score	5
Writeplacer Essay Structure	7
Creating Effective Thesis Statements	8
Thesis Statement – Exercises	9
Writing the Introduction	14
Writing the Introduction – Exercises	15
Organizing the Main Body	18
Elaboration in the Body Paragraphs	19
Elaboration of Supporting Points – Exercises	20
Using Linking Words and Subordination to Build Sentences	24
Using Linking Words and Subordination to Build Sentences – Exercises	31
Writing the Main Body Paragraphs – Exercises	42
Sample Main Body Paragraphs	46
Writing Clear and Concise Topic Sentences	49
Topic Sentences – Exercises	51
Writing the Conclusion	55
Writing the Conclusion – Exercises	56
Using Correct Grammar and Punctuation	61
Using Correct Grammar and Punctuation – Exercises	68
The Importance of Vocabulary for the Writeplacer – Using the Academic Word List	70
Academic Word List	71
Sample Essays and Exercises	78

ADVANTAGE+ EDITION – BONUS MATERIAL

Essay Correction Exercises:

Essay 1	83
Essay 2	90
Essay 3	97
Essay 4	103
Essay 5	110 |//
Answers to the Essay Correction Exercises	115

Writeplacer Essay Format & Question Types

Writeplacer assessment

Your Accuplacer testing assessment may include a written essay. This written essay is called the Writeplacer.

The purpose of the essay is to assess your ability to express your thoughts in a reasoned and academic manner.

The Writeplacer assesses this skill because academic writing is essential for success at college.

If you perform poorly on your Writeplacer essay, you may need to take a developmental English class during your freshman year.

Developmental English classes cost time and money. You may need to pay extra fees to enroll in this type of class, and the class is non-credit, so it won't count towards your degree.

Test administration

You will write your essay on a computer. Scratch paper will be available for you to take notes and plan your essay. Study aids, such as dictionaries or grammar books, are not permitted.

Time limit

You should ask your college about the time limit that they have established for the Writeplacer essay. Normally, you will be given one to two hours to plan, write, and edit your essay.

Word count

Your Writeplacer essay should be between 300 and 600 words.

Question types

Writeplacer essay questions can be classified into two general groups.

The first type of essay question includes a thought-provoking quotation on a topic and a related assignment which elicits your position on the topic.

Here is an example of a type 1 essay question:

Passage – "The only power any government has is the power to crack down on criminals. Well, when there aren't enough criminals, one makes them. One declares so many things to be a crime that it becomes impossible for men to live without breaking laws." Ayn Rand

Assignment – Illegal activity should be overlooked when doing so brings benefits to society at large.

The second type of essay question that you may encounter will ask you to describe your thoughts on a more personal topic, such as dilemmas commonly faced by students or by the individual in society.

Here is an example of a type 2 essay question:

Most Americans have access to computers and cell phones on a daily basis, making email and text messaging extremely popular. While some people argue that email and texting are now the most convenient forms of personal communication, others believe that electronic communication technology is often used inappropriately. Write an essay for an audience of educated adults in which you take a position on this topic. Be sure to provide reasons and examples to support your viewpoint.

We will see sample responses to these two essay topics in the subsequent sections.

Writeplacer Scoring – How the Automated Scoring Software Works

Your Writeplacer essay will be given a score from 1 to 8. The only exceptions are if a student writes an essay on a topic other than the one assigned or if the student writes in a language other than English; in these cases, a score of 0 will be given.

The Writeplacer has software that automatically scores your essay immediately after you click the "submit" button. You will receive your essay score and comments on the computer screen.

The six following characteristics of your essay will be assessed:

1. <u>Focus and purpose</u> – This means that your essay should answer the question that has been posed. You will need to express your main idea in a clear way in the introduction of the essay.

    The software assesses this aspect of your essay by searching for a thesis statement in the first paragraph of your essay.

2. <u>Organization</u> – Your essay should be divided into paragraphs, which have been set out in an organized manner. Each body paragraph should contain a point that supports your main idea. You should also include a conclusion that sums up the essay.

    The software looks for logical paragraph divisions, as well as for linking words and phrases which indicate that a new paragraph is beginning.

3. <u>Development and support</u> – It is extremely important to elaborate on the main idea of your essay and maintain your point of view throughout your writing. Your essay should include examples and explanations that illustrate and support your viewpoint. Remember that if your essay topic presents a contentious issue, you need to take a stance on only one side, rather than stating both the pro's and con's.

    The scoring software searches for linking words and phrases that signal that examples or reasons are being provided in the essay. These linking words and phrases include the following: such as, for example, for this reason, because of.

4. <u>Sentence construction</u> – You should write long and developed sentences that demonstrate a variety of sentence patterns. You should avoid repeatedly beginning your sentences in the same way, such as "I think that."

    The software is designed to search for a variety of sentence patterns.

5. <u>Mechanics</u> – Your essay should be grammatically accurate and punctuated correctly. Your spelling should also be correct.

    The software has an advanced grammar and spelling checker.

6. <u>Critical thinking</u> – Your essay should demonstrate unity and coherence among the examples that you use to support your argument. Students sometimes worry about the point of view that they decide to take. However, you will not be assessed on your opinions themselves, but rather on how well you have expressed, organized, and supported them.

   As mentioned in point 3 above, the software searches for linking words and phrases that introduce reasons and examples.

   In addition, the software checks your vocabulary level because, generally speaking, using an advanced level of academic vocabulary demonstrates that your thinking is complex and critical.

All of the above skills are covered in the subsequent sections of this study guide.

How to Avoid Common Writeplacer Errors and Raise Your Score

In the previous section, we talked about the characteristics of a well-written Writeplacer essay. However, you may also wonder which aspects of an essay would be scored poorly by the Writeplacer automated scoring software.

These errors most commonly cause students to receive a low Writeplacer score:

1. The essay fails to express a clear point of view or provides a viewpoint that cannot be logically supported.

   Tip: You can avoid this error by giving a clear thesis statement in the first paragraph of your essay.

2. The essay is written in a tone and style that is not suitable for an academic audience.

   Tip: Achieving the correct tone and style means that you need to avoid using informal or conversational expressions in your writing. Examples of informal language include words like "awesome" or "guy."

3. The reasons or examples provided in the essay are flawed because they do not support the student's main point.

   Tip: Be sure that your reasons and examples are closely related to your main idea and to the essay topic. For instance, if you are asked whether art programs should be supported in schools, and then go on to talk about physical education programs because you believe they are similar to art programs, your reasoning would be flawed.

4. The essay is disorganized and therefore difficult for the software to read and score.

   Tip: You can avoid this error by brainstorming your ideas and planning your essay before you begin writing.

5. The essay contains errors in sentence construction or contains only simple or repetitive sentence structures.

   Tip: Try to avoid writing every sentence of your essay in the subject-verb-object sentence pattern. In order to avoid this shortcoming, you can begin sentences with words and phrases like "although" or "because of this."

6. The essay does not demonstrate a complex thought process.

   Tip: Be sure that you give persuasive reasons and examples to express and support your position. Ensure that you have used academic vocabulary to express your ideas.

7. The essay analyzes information contained in the quotation, rather than in the assignment.

    Tip: Remember that the quotation is designed to be a thought-provoking aid for the assignment. You can refer back to the quotation to drive home a point that you are making in your essay, but you should not analyze the quotation in depth.

8. The essay contains errors in spelling, grammar, and punctuation.

    Tip: If you have weaknesses in these areas, you should spend more time studying the "Using Correct Grammar and Punctuation" section of this study guide.

Writeplacer Essay Structure

Most teachers agree that the best Writeplacer essays follow a four or five paragraph format. This format will help to insure that your essay is well-organized.

This format also helps you write longer and more developed essays that will be closer to 500 or 600 words, instead of just managing the 300-word minimum.

The five paragraph essay is organized as follows:

Paragraph 1 – This paragraph is the introduction to your essay. It should include a thesis statement that clearly indicates your main idea. It should also give the reader an overview of your supporting points.

Paragraph 2 – The second paragraph is where you elaborate on your first supporting point. It is normally recommended that you state your strongest and most persuasive point in this paragraph.

Paragraph 3 – You should elaborate on your main idea in the third paragraph by providing a second supporting point.

Paragraph 4 – You should mention your third supporting point in the fourth paragraph. This can be the supporting point that you feel to be the weakest.

Paragraph 5 – In the fifth and final paragraph of the essay, you should make your conclusion. The conclusion should reiterate your supporting points and sum up your position.

The four paragraph essay will follow the same structure as above, with paragraphs 2 and 3 elaborating two key supporting points and paragraph 4 stating the conclusion.

If you decide to put four paragraphs in your essay instead of five, each paragraph should be longer and slightly more detailed than that of a five paragraph essay.

We will illustrate both the four and five paragraph essay formats in our sample essays in the subsequent units of this study guide.

If you wish to skip ahead to a particular section, please refer to the Table of Contents to see which chapters cover each of the above skills.

Creating Effective Thesis Statements

<u>What is a thesis statement?</u>

A thesis statement is a sentence which asserts the main idea of your essay. The thesis statement is placed in the first paragraph of your essay.

Most essays on the Writeplacer will be on debatable or contentious topics. You will not need to write about both sides of the argument for the given topic. You only need to state which side of the argument you support and give reasons for your viewpoint.

<u>Write it early</u>

It is important to draft your thesis statement early in the writing process so that your writing has focus. However, be prepared to go back and edit your thesis statement after you have finished the main body of your essay.

<u>Keep it focused</u>

Remember that the best thesis statements are those that contain a central idea that will serve to narrow the focus of the essay and control the flow ideas within it. As such, a thesis statement should not be too general or vague.

<u>The "Assertion + Reason" Structure</u>

A good structure for the thesis statement is to think of it in terms of an assertion plus a reason or explanation. This structure is better than just giving your assertion or opinion on its own because your explanation indicates the direction that your writing is going to take.

In addition, the "assertion + reason" structure will result in a thesis statement that contains more words and which is usually richer grammatically and structurally. The scoring software is designed to assess these grammatical and structural aspects of your thesis statement.

Bearing these tips in mind, you should now complete the thesis statement exercises on the following pages.

Thesis Statement – Exercise 1

Now let's consider the essay topic we have seen earlier:

Passage – "The only power any government has is the power to crack down on criminals. Well, when there aren't enough criminals, one makes them. One declares so many things to be a crime that it becomes impossible for men to live without breaking laws." Ayn Rand

Assignment – Sometimes society should turn a blind eye to illegal activity.

Consider the following thesis statements for the above essay topic. Which one do you think is best? Why? Remember to consider focus and structure.

1. Illegal activity, such as entering a country without proper permission from the authorities, should normally be avoided.

2. While there is credence to the notion that laws should normally be obeyed, illegal activity should be overlooked when it serves as a catalyst for social and legal reform.

3. If illegal activity is ignored, then some possible benefits might come out of it to society as a whole.

4. Living in a lawless society is never a good idea.

Please use the area below to work out your response. The answer is provided on the next page.

Thesis Statement – Answer to Exercise 1

Analysis:

Thesis statement number 2 is the best example because is gives an assertion (illegal activity should be overlooked) and a reason (when it serves as a catalyst for social and legal reform). The reason given also shows that the essay will be focused, particularly on the idea of legal and social reform.

The sentence structure of answer number 2 is complex since it begins with a subordinator (*while*).

This answer also uses high-level academic vocabulary, such as the words "credence" and "catalyst."

Note that subordination and vocabulary are covered in subsequent sections of this study guide.

Answer 1 is not the best because gives an assertion (Illegal activity…should normally be avoided), but no reason.

Answer 3 gives an assertion (ignoring illegal activity) and a reason, but the reason is vague and unfocused because it talks about "some possible benefits," without stating precisely what the benefits are.

Answer 4 is not the best answer because it gives only a very broad assertion without providing any reason or explanation. Indeed, the concept of a lawless society as stated in answer 4 is even more general than that of an illegal activity, which was mentioned in answer 1. In addition, sentence 4 is much too short.

Thesis Statement – Exercise 2

Now look at the two essay topics below and write a focused thesis statement for each one, using the "Assertion + Reason" thesis statement structure.

1) Passage – "Three passions, simple but overwhelmingly strong, have governed my life: the longing for love, the search for knowledge, and unbearable pity for the suffering of mankind." Bertrand Russell

Assignment – Is it ever socially acceptable to be pleased when others suffer?

Your thesis statement:

2) Most Americans have access to computers and cell phones on a daily basis, making email and text messaging extremely popular. While some people argue that email and texting are now the most convenient forms of personal communication, others believe that electronic communication technology is often used inappropriately. Write an essay for an audience of educated adults in which you take a position on this topic. Be sure to provide reasons and examples to support your viewpoint.

Your thesis statement:

Thesis Statement – Answer to Exercise 2

1) Passage – "Three passions, simple but overwhelmingly strong, have governed my life: the longing for love, the search for knowledge, and unbearable pity for the suffering of mankind." Bertrand Russell

Assignment – Is it ever socially acceptable to be pleased when others suffer?

Suggested answer: Although being pleased to see others stricken is normally not acceptable in a civilized society, there are exceptions to this general rule when others have broken the society's norms during times of war or when a criminal is to be punished for his or her wrongdoing.

Analysis: The response is focused and controlled since it involves two precise and clearly-stated examples: war and crime.

The assertion is that "Although being pleased to see others stricken is normally not acceptable in a civilized society, there are exceptions to this general rule."

The reasons are "when others have broken the society's norms during times of war or when a criminal is to be punished for his or her wrongdoing."

Notice that the response avoids a common temptation to which students often succumb, namely, beginning their response with the exact wording of the assignment.

In other words, given the example above, you should avoid beginning your thesis statement with the phrase "It is sometimes socially acceptable to be pleased when others suffer because…" since the assignment question already contains the phrase "socially acceptable to be pleased when others suffer."

2) Most Americans have access to computers and cell phones on a daily basis, making email and text messaging extremely popular. While some people argue that email and texting are now the most convenient forms of personal communication, others believe that electronic communication technology is often used inappropriately. Write an essay for an audience of educated adults in which you take a position on this topic. Be sure to provide reasons and examples to support your viewpoint.

Suggested answer: Modern forms of communication such as electronic mail and SMS messaging can cause problems with personal relationships because of three main shortcomings with these media: their impersonal nature, their inability to capture tone and sarcasm, and their easy accessibility at times of anger.

Analysis: The assertion is that "Modern forms of communication such as electronic mail and SMS messaging can cause problems with personal relationships."

The reasons are "their impersonal nature, their inability to capture tone and sarcasm, and their easy accessibility at times of anger."

The essay will be focused because it will have three main body paragraphs, which will discuss in turn each of the reasons provided.

Writing the Introduction

What is the purpose of the introduction?

The purpose of your introduction is to give a brief statement of your point of view and to provide an overview of your supporting points.

What can I include in my introduction?

You can include a vivid example, an interesting fact, a paradoxical statement, or even a supporting anecdote in your introduction.

When should I write the introduction?

Although it is advisable to write your thesis statement before beginning your main body, you can often go back and write the remainder of the introduction after you have finished the body paragraphs and conclusion.

That is because sometimes it is easier to introduce your essay after you have already written it and developed your points.

What is the structure of the introduction?

You can think of the essay introduction like a funnel: wide at the top and narrow at the bottom. In other words, start off your introduction in a general but interesting way, and then narrow it down to your main idea and specific supporting points.

Remember that the introduction announces your main idea and supporting points, while your main body develops them.

Now complete the exercises on writing introductions on the following pages.

Writing the Introduction – Exercises

Look at our previous essay topics again and write an introduction of 100 to 140 words for each one. Remember to include a clear and focused thesis statement at the end of your introduction. Sample answers are provided on the following pages.

1) Passage – "Three passions, simple but overwhelmingly strong, have governed my life: the longing for love, the search for knowledge, and unbearable pity for the suffering of mankind." Bertrand Russell

Assignment – Is it ever socially acceptable to be pleased when others suffer?

Your introduction:

2) Most Americans have access to computers and cell phones on a daily basis, making email and text messaging extremely popular. While some people argue that email and texting are now the most convenient forms of personal communication, others believe that electronic communication technology is often used inappropriately. Write an essay for an audience of educated adults in which you take a position on this topic. Be sure to provide reasons and examples to support your viewpoint.

Your introduction:

Writing the Introduction – Answer 1

1) Passage – "Three passions, simple but overwhelmingly strong, have governed my life: the longing for love, the search for knowledge, and unbearable pity for the suffering of mankind." Bertrand Russell

Assignment – Is it ever socially acceptable to be pleased when others suffer?

While feeling pleasure when others suffer is a human emotion to which most of us would not be so quick to admit, there are occasions when it is socially acceptable to take pleasure in the pain of others. Consider, for example, the gratification that the people of European countries would have experienced when Hitler was defeated during the Second World War. Punishment for crime is another occasion where it is not considered untoward to experience satisfaction over the suffering of others. That is to say, although being pleased to see others stricken is normally not acceptable in a civilized society, there are exceptions to this general rule when others have broken the society's norms during times of war or when a criminal is to be punished for his or her wrongdoing.

Analysis:

The first sentence of the essay by introduces the topic in general.

The second sentence begins to create a specific focus to the essay by providing a vivid and relevant historical example.

The third sentence makes a transition to the thesis statement by introducing the second supporting example.

The fourth sentence of the introduction is the thesis statement, which was analyzed previously.

Writing the Introduction – Answer 2

2) Most Americans have access to computers and cell phones on a daily basis, making email and text messaging extremely popular. While some people argue that email and texting are now the most convenient forms of personal communication, others believe that electronic communication technology is often used inappropriately. Write an essay for an audience of educated adults in which you take a position on this topic. Be sure to provide reasons and examples to support your viewpoint.

Suggested answer:

There is no disputing the fact that email and SMS technologies have made our lives easier in a variety of ways. Nevertheless, many of us will have had the experience of falling out with a friend or loved one over an email or text message whose content was poorly written or misconstrued. Clearly, there are certain drawbacks to emails and texts since electronic messaging cannot capture the nuances and subtleties of verbal communication. Modern forms of communication such as electronic mail and SMS messaging can cause problems with personal relationships because of three main shortcomings with these media: their impersonal nature, their inability to capture tone and sarcasm, and their easy accessibility at times of anger.

Analysis:

The first sentence describes the effect of communication technology on daily life in general.

The second sentence provides an interesting anecdote because the account of having a disagreement with a loved one about the content of an email message is a universal experience.

The third sentence logically connects the example of miscommunication to the thesis statement.

The fourth sentence of the introduction is the thesis statement, which also contains the supporting points.

Organizing the Main Body

Each paragraph of your main body should consist of the following elements:

1. A topic sentence which concisely states the supporting point that you are going to discuss in the paragraph.

2. Well-written and complex sentences that elaborate on your supporting points through reasons and examples.

3. The use of subordination and linking words in order to create a variety of different types of sentence construction.

You may wish to write the body of the paragraph before writing your topic sentence for it because sometimes it is easier to sum up the main point of the paragraph after you have written it.

For this reason, we will next look at elaboration of supporting points and writing the main body sentences, before turning our attention to topic sentences.

Elaboration in the Body Paragraphs

How long should each body paragraph be?

For a four paragraph essay, each body paragraph should range from 120 to 170 words. For a five paragraph essay, each body paragraph should be from 100 to 140 words.

What is an elaborating idea?

Elaborating ideas include both explanations and examples. Providing clear examples to support your points is extremely important.

Each of your main body paragraphs should contain an example that supports your line of argument.

You should elaborate on and explain your example in order to make your essay persuasive.

How do elaborating ideas help to raise my Writeplacer score?

Elaboration lengthens your essay and gives you more opportunities to demonstrate higher-level grammar, complex sentence construction, and academic vocabulary.

These criteria (grammar, construction, and vocabulary) are easily detected by the Writeplacer scoring software.

How many elaborating ideas should I have in each paragraph?

This roughly equates to two or three elaborating ideas for each body paragraph.

How do I link my elaborating ideas to one another?

You should seamlessly link your elaborating points together to make a coherent paragraph.

This is the function of linking words and subordination, which we will cover in the next section.

How do I come up with elaborating ideas for each supporting point?

Perhaps the best way to elaborate on your supporting points is to take each of the supporting points that you are going to talk about in your main body paragraphs, place them as headings on a piece of scratch paper, and make a list of examples and explanations under each heading.

We will have a look at how to do this in the following exercise.

Elaboration of Supporting Points – Exercise 1

Now let's look at the introduction to our sample essay on the suffering of others:

> While feeling pleasure when others suffer is a human emotion to which most of us would not be so quick to admit, there are occasions when it is socially acceptable to take pleasure in the pain of others. Consider, for example, the gratification that the people of European countries would have experienced when Hitler was defeated during the Second World War. Punishment for crime is another occasion where it is not considered untoward to experience satisfaction over the suffering of others. That is to say, although being pleased to see others stricken is normally not acceptable in a civilized society, there are exceptions to this general rule when others have broken the society's norms during times of war or when a criminal is to be punished for his or her wrongdoing.

This will be a four paragraph essay, with two main body paragraphs. Body paragraph 1 will discuss World War II. Body paragraph 2 will discuss punishment for crime.

Remember not to be concerned about grammar and sentence construction when you make your list of elaborating points. Simply jot down ideas and phrases as they come to you. We will talk about improving your grammar and sentence construction in a subsequent section.

Exercise – Now try to make a list of the ideas you are going to use as elaboration for each of your main body paragraphs. Sample responses are on the next page.

Elaboration – Body Paragraph 1:

Elaboration – Body Paragraph 2:

Elaboration of Supporting Points – Answer to Exercise 1

You'll remember that the suggested introduction is as follows:

> While feeling pleasure when others suffer is a human emotion to which most of us would not be so quick to admit, there are occasions when it is socially acceptable to take pleasure in the pain of others. Consider, for example, the gratification that the people of European countries would have experienced when Hitler was defeated during the Second World War. Punishment for crime is another occasion where it is not considered untoward to experience satisfaction over the suffering of others. That is to say, although being pleased to see others stricken is normally not acceptable in a civilized society, there are exceptions to this general rule when others have broken the society's norms during times of war or when a criminal is to be punished for his or her wrongdoing.

Here are some possible elaborating points:

Elaboration – Body Paragraph 1:

Times of adversity during World War II

- Example: Adolph Hitler, dictator, heinous acts during WWII
- Hitler's cruelty – People fled their homes without possessions
- Death camps – Unthinkable states of existence
- The world was pleased when Hitler faced adversity
- Worldwide satisfaction when he was overthrown and surrendered

Elaboration – Body Paragraph 2:

The role of punishment in redressing the actions of criminals

- Criminal law – socially created – offenders tried and punished
- Satisfaction when justice is served
- Suffering may act as a deterrent to would-be criminals & reinforces social norms

Elaboration of Supporting Points – Exercise 2

Let's turn our attention to our sample essay on email and text communication.

You'll remember that the suggested introduction is as follows:

> There is no disputing the fact that email and SMS technologies have made our lives easier in a variety of ways. Nevertheless, many of us will have had the experience of falling out with a friend or loved one over an email or text message whose content was poorly written or misconstrued. Clearly, there are certain drawbacks to emails and texts since electronic messaging cannot capture the nuances and subtleties of verbal communication. Modern forms of communication such as electronic mail and SMS messaging can cause problems with personal relationships because of three main shortcomings with these media: their impersonal nature, their inability to capture tone and sarcasm, and their easy accessibility at times of anger.

This will be a five paragraph essay, so your in your first body paragraph you need to elaborate on the impersonal nature of electronic communication.

Your second body paragraph will elaborate on how emails and texts cannot convey tone and sarcasm.

The third paragraph will talk about the danger of having an accessible messaging service during times of high emotion.

Exercise – Now try to make a list of the ideas you are going to use as elaboration for each of your main body paragraphs. Sample responses are on the next page.

Elaboration – Body Paragraph 1:

Elaboration – Body Paragraph 2:

Elaboration – Body Paragraph 3:

Elaboration of Supporting Points – Answer to Exercise 2

Here is the introduction again for ease of reference:

> There is no disputing the fact that email and SMS technologies have made our lives easier in a variety of ways. Nevertheless, many of us will have had the experience of falling out with a friend or loved one over an email or text message whose content was poorly written or misconstrued. Clearly, there are certain drawbacks to emails and texts since electronic messaging cannot capture the nuances and subtleties of verbal communication. Modern forms of communication such as electronic mail and SMS messaging can cause problems with personal relationships because of three main shortcomings with these media: their impersonal nature, their inability to capture tone and sarcasm, and their easy accessibility at times of anger.

Elaboration – Body Paragraph 1:

Elaborate on the impersonal nature of electronic communication

- Email is practical, but not always appropriate. Example: informing someone about a death
- No human contact – can be seen as cold or shallow – not like talking on phone or in person

Elaboration – Body Paragraph 2:

Emails and texts cannot convey tone and sarcasm

- It is possible for sarcastic comments to be taken literally
- Message clear to sender, but tone of emotion is conveyed by voice
- Without tone, may come across as demanding, indifferent, etc.

Elaboration – Body Paragraph 3:

The danger of having an accessible messaging service during times of high emotion

- Examples: breaking up with someone by text; firing someone by email
- Easy to send a message quickly when angry – can hurt relationships – waiting and thinking requires self-control & discipline

Using Linking Words and Subordination to Build Sentences

In order to perform well on the Writeplacer exam, you will need to write long and developed sentences.

Sentence linking words can help you combine short sentences together to create more complex sentence structures.

Sentence linking words and phrases fall into three categories: sentence linkers, phrase linkers, and subordinators.

In order to understand how to use these types of sentence linking words and phrases correctly, you will need to know some basics of English grammar.

The basic grammatical principles for these concepts are explained in this section. Be sure to study the examples carefully before you attempt the exercises in the following sections of the study guide.

TYPE 1 – SENTENCE LINKERS:

Sentence linkers are used to link two complete sentences together. A complete sentence is one that has a grammatical subject and a verb.

Sentence linkers are usually placed at the beginning of a sentence and are followed by a comma.

They can also be preceded by a semicolon and followed by a comma when joining two sentences together. When doing so, the first letter of the first word of the second sentence must not be capitalized.

Sentence linker examples:

You need to enjoy your time at college. *However*, you should still study hard.

You need to enjoy your time at college; *however*, you should still study hard.

In the examples above, the grammatical subject of the first sentence is "you" and the verb is "need to enjoy".

In the second sentence, "you" is the grammatical subject and "should study" is the verb.

TYPE 2 – PHRASE LINKERS:

In order to understand the difference between phrase linkers and sentence linkers, you must first be able to distinguish a sentence from a phrase.

A phrase linker must be followed by a phrase, while a sentence linker must be followed by a sentence.

The basic distinction between phrases and sentences is that phrases do not have both grammatical subjects and verbs, while sentences contain grammatical subjects and verbs.

Here are some examples of phrases:

Her beauty and grace

Life's little problems

A lovely summer day in the month of June

Working hard

Being desperate for money

Note that the last two phrases above use the –ing form, known in these instances as the present participle.

Present participle phrases, which are often used to modify nouns or pronouns, are sometimes placed at the beginning of sentences as introductory phrases.

Here are some examples of sentences:

Mary worked all day long.

My sister lives in Seattle.

Wintertime is brutal in Montana.

"Mary," "my sister," and "wintertime" are the grammatical subjects of the above sentences.

Remember that verbs are words that show action or states of being, so "worked," "lives," and "is" are the verbs in the three sentences above.

Look at the examples that follow:

<u>Phrase linker example 1 – no comma:</u> He received a promotion *because of* his dedication to the job.

"His dedication to the job" is a noun phrase.

<u>Phrase linker example 2 – with comma:</u> *Because of* his dedication to the job, he received a promotion.

When the sentence begins with the phrase linker, we classify the sentence as an inverted sentence.

Notice that you will need to place a comma between the two parts of the sentence when it is inverted.

TYPE 3 – SUBORDINATORS:

Subordinators must be followed by an independent clause. Subordinators cannot be followed by a phrase.

The two clauses of a subordinated sentence must be separated by a comma.

The structure of independent clauses is similar to that of sentences because independent clauses contain a grammatical subject and a verb.

Subordinator examples:

Although he worked hard, he failed to make his business profitable.

He failed to make his business profitable, *although* he worked hard.

There are two clauses: "He worked hard" and "he failed to make his business profitable."

The grammatical subjects in each clause are the words "he", while the verbs are "worked" and "failed."

Now look at the sentence linking words and phrases below. Note which ones are sentence linkers, which ones are phrase linkers, and which ones are subordinators.

Then refer to the rules above to remember the grammatical principles for sentence linkers, phrase linkers, and subordinators.

Sentence linkers for giving additional information

further

furthermore

apart from this

what is more

in addition

additionally

in the same way

moreover

Sentence linkers for giving examples

for example

for instance

in this case

in particular

more precisely

namely

in brief

in short

Sentence linkers for stating the obvious

obviously

clearly

naturally

of course

surely

after all

Sentence linkers for giving generalizations

in general

on the whole

as a rule

for the most part

generally speaking

in most cases

Sentence linkers for stating causes and effects

thus

accordingly

hence

therefore

in that case

under those circumstances

as a result

for this reason

as a consequence

consequently

in effect

Sentence linkers for concession or unexpected results

however

nevertheless

meanwhile

Sentence linkers for giving conclusions

finally

to conclude

lastly

in conclusion

Sentence linkers for contrast

on the other hand

on the contrary

alternatively

rather

Sentence linkers for paraphrasing or restating

in other words

that is to say

that is

Sentence linkers for showing similarity

similarly

in the same way

likewise

Phrase linkers for giving additional information

besides

in addition to

Phrase linkers for stating causes and effects

because of

due to

owing to

Phrase linkers for concession or unexpected results

despite

in spite of

Phrase linkers for comparison

compared to

like

Phrase linkers for contrast

in contrast to

instead of

rather than

without

Subordinators

although

as

because

but

due to the fact that

even though

since

so

so that

once

unless

until

when

whereas

while

not only . . . but also

Time words that can be used both as phrase linkers and subordinators

after

before

Special cases

yet – "Yet" can be used as both a subordinator and as a sentence linker.

in order to – "In order to" must be followed by the base form of the verb.

thereby – "Thereby" must be followed by the present participle.

We will look at the present participle and base forms in the exercises in this section.

Using Linking Words and Subordination to Build Sentences – Exercises

Look at the pairs of sentences in the exercises below. Make new sentences, using the phrase linkers, sentence linkers, and subordinators provided. In many cases, you will need to create one single sentence from the two sentences provided. You may need to change or delete some of the words in the original sentences.

We will return to our two sample essay topics after this exercise.

Exercise 1:

The temperature was quite high yesterday.

It really didn't feel that hot outside.

Write new sentences beginning as follows:

a) In spite of . . .

Hint: You need to change the form of the verb "was" in answer (a).

b) The temperature . . .

You need to include the word "nevertheless" in answer (b). Be careful with punctuation and capitalization in your answer.

Exercise 2:

Our star athlete didn't receive a gold medal in the Olympics.

He had trained for competition for several years in advance.

Write new sentences beginning as follows:

a) Our star athlete . . . .

Answer (a) should contain the word "although."

b) Despite . . .

Exercise 3:

There are acrimonious relationships within our extended family.

Our immediate family decided to go away on vacation during the holiday season to avoid these conflicts.

Write new sentences beginning as follows:

a) Because of . . .

b) Because . . .

c) Due to the fact that . . .

Exercise 4:

My best friend had been feeling extremely sick for several days.

She refused to see the doctor.

Write new sentences beginning as follows:

a) My best friend . . .

Answer (a) should contain the word "however."

b) My best friend . . .

Answer (b) should contain the word "but."

Be careful with capitalization and punctuation in your answers.

Exercise 5:

He generally doesn't like drinking alcohol.

He will do so on social occasions.

Write new sentences beginning as follows:

a) While . . .

b) He generally . . .

Answer (b) should contain the word "yet."

Exercise 6:

The government's policies failed to stimulate spending and expand economic growth.

The country slipped further into recession.

Write new sentences beginning as follows:

a) The government's policies . . .

Answer (a) should contain the word "thus."

b) The government's policies . . .

Answer (b) should contain the word "so."

Exercise 7:

Students may attend certain classes without fulfilling a prerequisite.

Students are advised of the benefit of taking at least one non-required introductory course.

Write new sentences beginning as follows:

a) Even though . . .

b) Students may attend . . .

Answer (b) should contain the phrase "apart from this."

Exercise 8:

There have been advances in technology and medical science.

Infant mortality rates have declined substantially in recent years.

Write new sentences beginning as follows:

a) Owing to . . .

b) Since . . .

Exercise 9:

It was the most expensive restaurant in town.

It had rude staff and provided the worst service.

Write new sentences beginning as follows:

a) It was the most . . .

Answer (a) should contain the word "besides."

b) In addition to . . .

Exercise 10:

Now try to combine these three sentences:

The judge did not punish the criminal justly.

He decided to grant a lenient sentence.

He did not send out a message to deter potential offenders in the future.

Write new sentences as follows:

a) Instead of . . . and thereby . . .

b) Rather than . . . in order to . . .

Before you attempt your answer, look for the cause and effect relationships among the three sentences.

In other words, which event came first? Which ones were second and third in the chain of events?

Also be careful with punctuation in your answers.

Using Linking Words and Subordination to Build Sentences – Answers

Exercise 1:

The temperature was quite high yesterday.

It really didn't feel that hot outside.

Answer (a):

a) In spite of the temperature being quite high yesterday, it really didn't feel that hot outside.

The words "in spite of" are a phrase linker, not a sentence linker.

That is to say, "in spite of" needs to be followed by a phrase, not a clause.

The verb "was" needs to be changed to "being" in order to form a present participle phrase.

Present participle phrases are made by using the –ing form of the verb. We will see this construction again in some of the following answers.

Answer (b):

There are two possible answers:

b) The temperature was quite high yesterday. Nevertheless, it really didn't feel that hot outside.

b) The temperature was quite high yesterday; nevertheless, it really didn't feel that hot outside.

"Nevertheless" is a sentence linker. As such, it needs to be used to begin a new sentence.

Alternatively, the semicolon can be used to join the original sentences. If the semicolon is used, the first letter of the word following it must not be capitalized.

Exercise 2:

Our star athlete didn't receive a gold medal in the Olympics.

He had trained for competition for several years in advance.

Answer (a):

a) Our star athlete didn't receive a gold medal in the Olympics, although he had trained for competition for several years in advance

"Although" is a subordinator, so the two sentences can be combined without any changes.

Answer (b):

b) Despite having trained for competition for several years in advance, our star athlete didn't receive a gold medal in the Olympics.

"Despite" is a phrase linker. As we have seen in answer (a) of exercise 1 above, phrase linkers need to be followed by phrases, not clauses.

The two parts of the sentence are inverted, and the verb "had" needs to be changed to "having" to make the present participle form.

Exercise 3:

There are acrimonious relationships within our extended family.

Our immediate family decided to go away on vacation during the holiday season to avoid these conflicts.

Answer (a):

a) Because of acrimonious relationships within our extended family, our immediate family decided to go away on vacation during the holiday season to avoid these conflicts.

"Because of" is a phrase linker. As such, the subject and verb (there are) need to be removed from the original sentence in order to form a phrase.

Answer (b):

b) Because there are acrimonious relationships within our extended family, our immediate family decided to go away on vacation during the holiday season to avoid these conflicts.

Answer (c):

c) Due to the fact that there are acrimonious relationships within our extended family, our immediate family decided to go away on vacation during the holiday season to avoid these conflicts.

"Because" and "due to the fact that" are subordinators, so no changes to the original sentences are required.

The phrase "to avoid these conflicts" can be omitted since this idea is already implied by the words "acrimonious relationships."

Exercise 4:

My best friend had been feeling extremely sick for several days.

She refused to see the doctor.

Answer (a):

There are two possible answers.

a) My best friend had been feeling extremely sick for several days. However, she refused to see the doctor.

a) My best friend had been feeling extremely sick for several days; however, she refused to see the doctor.

Like "nevertheless" in exercise 1, the word "however" is a sentence linker. Remember that sentence linkers need to be used at the beginning of a new sentence.

Alternatively, the semicolon can be used to join the original sentences. If the semicolon is used, "however" must not begin with a capital letter and needs to be followed by a comma.

Answer (b):

b) My best friend had been feeling extremely sick for several days, but she refused to see the doctor.

"But" is a subordinator, so the two sentences can be combined without any changes.

Exercise 5:

He generally doesn't like drinking alcohol.

He will do so on social occasions.

Answer (a):

a) While he generally doesn't like drinking alcohol, he will do so on social occasions.

Like "although," the word "while" is a subordinator, so no changes to the original sentences are needed.

Answer (b):

"Yet" can be used as both a subordinator and as a sentence linker, so there are three possible answers in this instance.

When used as a sentence linker, the sentence construction is similar to the sentences containing nevertheless" from exercise 1 and "however" from exercise 4.

Accordingly, these are two possible answers:

b) He doesn't like drinking alcohol. Yet, he will do so on social occasions.

b) He doesn't like drinking alcohol; yet, he will do so on social occasions.

A third possible answer is to use "yet" as a subordinator:

b) He doesn't like drinking alcohol, yet he will do so on social occasions.

The difference is that the third sentence places slightly less emphasis on the particular occasions in which he will drink than the other two sentences.

Exercise 6:

The government's policies failed to stimulate spending and expand economic growth.

The country slipped further into recession.

Answer (a):

"Thus" is a sentence linker, so there are two possible answers:

a) The government's policies failed to stimulate spending and expand economic growth. Thus, the country slipped further into recession.

a) The government's policies failed to stimulate spending and expand economic growth; thus, the country slipped further into recession.

Answer (b):

b) The government's policies failed to stimulate spending and expand economic growth, so the country slipped further into recession.

"So" is a subordinator. The two sentences may therefore be joined without any changes.

Exercise 7:

Students may attend certain classes without fulfilling a prerequisite.

Students are advised of the benefit of taking at least one non-required introductory course.

Answer (a):

There are two possible answers.

a) Even though students may attend certain classes without fulfilling a prerequisite, they are advised of the benefit of taking at least one non-required introductory course.

a) Even though students are advised of the benefit of taking at least one non-required introductory course, they may attend certain classes without fulfilling a prerequisite.

"Even though" is a subordinator, so no changes are needed. It is advisable to change the word "students" to the pronoun "they" on the second part of the new sentence in order to avoid repetition.

The order or the clauses may be changed in the new sentence since there is no cause and effect relationship between the two original sentences.

Answer (b):

There are two possible answers:

b) Students may attend certain classes without fulfilling a prerequisite. Apart from this, they are advised of the benefit of taking at least one non-required introductory course.

b) Students may attend certain classes without fulfilling a prerequisite; apart from this, they are advised of the benefit of taking at least one non-required introductory course.

"Apart from this" is a sentence linker, so it needs to be used at the beginning of a separate sentence.

Exercise 8:

There have been advances in technology and medical science.

Infant mortality rates have declined substantially in recent years.

Answer (a):

a) Owing to advances in technology and medical science, infant mortality rates have declined substantially in recent years.

"Owing to" is a phrase linker that shows cause and effect. In this case the cause is advances in technology and medical science, and the effect or result is the decline in infant mortality rates.

Since "owing to" is a phrase linker, the grammatical subject of the original sentence (there) and the verb (have been) are removed when creating the new sentence.

Answer (b):

b) Since there have been advances in technology and medical science, infant mortality rates have declined substantially in recent years.

"Since" is a subordinator, so you can combine the sentences without making any changes.

Remember to use the comma between the two parts of the sentence because the clauses have been inverted.

Exercise 9:

It was the most expensive restaurant in town.

It had rude staff and provided the worst service.

Answer (a):

a) It was the most expensive restaurant in town, besides having rude staff and providing the worst service.

"Besides" is a phrase linker, so use the present participle form of both verbs in the second original sentence. Accordingly, "had" becomes "having" and "provide" becomes "providing."

Answer (b):

There are two possible answers.

b) In addition to being the most expensive restaurant in town, it had rude staff and provided the worst service.

b) In addition to having rude staff and providing the worst service, it was the most expensive restaurant in town.

"In addition to" is a phrase linker, so the present participle forms are used in the phrase containing this word.

The order of the original sentences can be changed since there is no cause and effect relationship between these ideas.

Exercise 10:

Now try to combine these three sentences:

The judge did not punish the criminal justly.

He decided to grant a lenient sentence.

He did not send out a message to deter potential offenders in the future.

Answer (a):

a) Instead of punishing the criminal justly and thereby sending out a message to deter potential offenders in the future, the judge decided to grant a lenient sentence.

Answer (b):

b) Rather than punishing the criminal justly in order to send out a message to deter potential offenders in the future, the judge decided to grant a lenient sentence.

As you will see, answers A and B are somewhat similar in their construction.

"Instead of" and "rather than" need to be used with the present particle form (punishing).

"Thereby" must be followed by the present participle form (sending).

However, "in order to" needs to take the base form of the verb (send).

The base form is the verb before any change has been made to it, like making the –ed or –ing forms. The following are examples of base forms of verbs: eat, sleep, work, play.

Writing the Main Body Paragraphs – Essay 1 Exercise

We had a look at brainstorming ideas for your main body paragraphs in a previous section of this study guide.

We will now return to the ideas we developed in that section and write the paragraphs of the main body of our essays.

We will also need the skills we have practiced in the sentence building section in order to use sentence linking words and subordination to write in an organized way.

Remember that while sentence linking words and subordination are important because they give an essay cohesion and structure, you should avoid using a sentence linker or subordinator in every sentence of your essay.

That is because the Writeplacer scoring software searches for a variety of sentence patterns in your writing.

Accordingly, some of the sentences in our model answer will have linking words and subordinators, although others will not.

Within each exercise, we reproduce our list of elaborating points for the body paragraphs for ease of reference.

Main Body Paragraph 1:

Times of adversity during World War II

- Example: Adolph Hitler, dictator, heinous acts during WWII
- Hitler's cruelty – People fled their homes without possessions
- Death camps – Unthinkable states of existence
- The world was pleased when Hitler faced adversity
- Worldwide satisfaction when he was overthrown and surrendered

Now write the sentences for main body paragraphs, excluding the topic sentence. Some words from the basic sentence structure of the sample response are provided in order to guide you. Refer to the lists above each exercise to help you. Write each new sentence in the order of the points provided above.

Sentence 1: Adolph Hitler, arguably . . . , committed . . . during World War II.

Sentence 2: Due to his atrocities, previously contented residents . . . , leaving behind . . .

Sentence 3: The most unfortunate . . . submitted to unthinkable states of existence . . . that Hitler oversaw.

Sentence 4: Because they were forced . . . , those that Hitler persecuted . . .

Sentence 5: Once Hitler had encountered the final ultimatum of surrender . . ., the relief and satisfaction . . .

Main Body Paragraph 2:

The role of punishment in redressing the actions of criminals

- Criminal law – socially created – offenders tried and punished
- Satisfaction when justice is served
- Suffering may act as a deterrent to would-be criminals & reinforces social norms

Sentence 1: Criminal law, which has been created . . . , has been established to ensure that offenders . . .

Sentence 2: When someone has broken the norms . . . , other members of the community feel satisfied because . . .

Sentence 3: In addition, punishing social wrongs . . . , thereby . . .

Writing the Main Body Paragraphs – Essay 2 Exercise

Now write the sentences for main body paragraphs for essay 2, excluding the topic sentence. Some words from the basic sentence structure of the sample response are provided in order to guide you. Refer to the lists above each exercise to help you. Write each new sentence in the order of the points provided

The elaborating points for essay 2 are provided again for ease of reference.

Main Body Paragraph 1:

Elaborate on the impersonal nature of electronic communication

- Email is practical, but not always appropriate. Example: informing someone about a death
- No human contact – can be seen as cold or shallow – not like talking on phone or in person

Sentence 1: Although email may be practical for . . . , electronic messaging would be remarkably inappropriate for . . .

Sentence 2: There is no direct human contact in . . . , and during times of loss or tragedy, human warmth . . .

Main Body Paragraph 2:

Emails and texts cannot convey tone and sarcasm

- It is possible for sarcastic comments to be taken literally
- Message clear to sender, but tone of emotion is conveyed by voice
- Without tone, may come across as demanding, indifferent, etc.

Sentence 1: For instance, it might be possible . . . of a sarcastic email message to . . .

Sentence 2: The tone of . . . may seem abundantly clear to . . . , but sarcastic or ironically humorous utterances can only . . .

Sentence 3: Without . . . , certain phrases in an email may . . .

Main Body Paragraph 3:

The danger of having an accessible messaging service during times of high emotion

- Examples: breaking up with someone by text; firing someone by email
- Easy to send a message quickly when angry – can hurt relationships – waiting and thinking requires self-control & discipline

Sentence 1: In this day and age, we have heard stories not only of . . . , but also of employers who . . .

Sentence 2: Unless the writer of the message has . . . before . . . , he or she might send a regrettable message that can . . .

Sample Main Body Paragraphs – Essay 1

Our list of elaborating points for the body paragraphs in essay 1 was as follows:

Elaboration – Body Paragraph 1:

Times of adversity during World War II

- Example: Adolph Hitler, dictator, heinous acts during WWII
- Hitler's cruelty – People fled their homes without possessions
- Death camps – Unthinkable states of existence
- The world was pleased when Hitler faced adversity
- Worldwide satisfaction when he was overthrown and surrendered

Sample Body Paragraph 1 (excluding topic sentence):

Adolph Hitler, arguably the most notorious dictator of the twentieth century, committed countless heinous acts against the inhabitants of several European countries during World War II. Due to his atrocities, previously contented residents of many towns and villages had to flee their homes in fear, leaving behind all of their worldly possessions. The most unfortunate of these persecuted individuals were submitted to unthinkable states of existence in the many death camps that Hitler oversaw. Because they were forced to live in such unimaginable conditions, those that Hitler persecuted must have been gratified when the dictator faced adversity during the war. Once Hitler had encountered the final ultimatum of surrender or death and his regime was overthrown, the relief and satisfaction openly expressed around the world on a personal level was immense.

Elaboration – Body Paragraph 2:

The role of punishment in redressing the actions of criminals

- Criminal law – socially created – offenders tried and punished
- Satisfaction when justice is served
- Suffering may act as a deterrent to would-be criminals & reinforces social norms

Sample Body Paragraph 2 (excluding topic sentence):

Criminal law, which has been created according to traditional social convention, has been established to ensure that offenders will be justly tried and punished for their crimes. When someone has broken the norms of society in this way, other members of the community feel satisfied because they believe that justice has been served when the offender has been punished. In addition, punishing social wrongs can act as a deterrent to would-be criminals, thereby further reinforcing social norms.

Sample Main Body Paragraphs – Essay 2

Here are the elaborating points for essay 2 again for ease of reference:

Elaboration – Body Paragraph 1:

Elaborate on the impersonal nature of electronic communication

- Email is practical, but not always appropriate. Example: informing someone about a death
- No human contact – can be seen as cold or shallow – not like talking on phone or in person

Sample Body Paragraph 1 (excluding topic sentence):

Although email may be practical for conveying straightforward information or facts, electronic messaging would be remarkably inappropriate for events like announcing a death. There is no direct human contact in emails and texts, and during times of loss or tragedy, human warmth and depth of emotion can only truly be conveyed through a phone call, or better still, by talking face to face.

Elaboration – Body Paragraph 2:

Emails and texts cannot convey tone and sarcasm

- It is possible for sarcastic comments to be taken literally
- Message clear to sender, but tone of emotion is conveyed by voice
- Without tone, may come across as demanding, indifferent, etc.

Sample Body Paragraph 2 (excluding topic sentence):

For instance, it might be possible for the recipient of a sarcastic email message to take its contents literally. The tone of the message may seem abundantly clear to the person who sent it, but sarcastic or ironically humorous utterances can only really be communicated in speech through the tone and inflection of the voice. Without the aid of tone and inflection, certain phrases in an email may come across as demanding, indifferent, or rude.

Elaboration – Body Paragraph 3:

The danger of having an accessible messaging service during times of high emotion

- Examples: breaking up with someone by text; firing someone by email
- Easy to send a message quickly when angry – can hurt relationships – waiting and thinking requires self-control & discipline

Sample Main Body Paragraphs – Essay 2

Sample Body Paragraph 3 (excluding topic sentence):

In this day and age, we have heard stories not only of personal break ups that have been conducted by text, but also of employers who fire their staff by email message. Unless the writer of the message has the discipline and self-control to give him or herself a period of reasoned contemplation before sending the communication, he or she might send a regrettable message that can cause irretrievable damage to a relationship.

Writing Clear and Concise Topic Sentences

Why are topic sentences important?

As the Writeplacer software moves into each new paragraph of your essay, it will look for new ideas by searching for words and phrases that you have not used previously in your writing.

Each topic sentence should therefore paraphrase, *but not repeat word for word*, the supporting points in your thesis statement.

What is the purpose of a topic sentence?

You can think of the topic sentence as a summary of the content of a main body paragraph. The topic sentence serves two purposes.

First of all, it gives an overview of the content of the paragraph because it announces the topic that you are going to discuss.

Secondly, the topic sentence links back to the thesis statement since it is an elaboration of one of the supporting points that you have already cited at the beginning of the essay.

In this way, clear and concise topic sentences give your essay cohesion and coherence.

Is a topic sentence general or specific in its focus?

While the topic sentence is more specific than the thesis statement, the topic sentence should be more general than the elaboration that you are going to make in the paragraph.

In other words, in the same way that your introductory paragraph moves from a general idea to more specific ones, so too does each main body paragraph move from the more general supporting point that you mention in your topic sentence to the specific points that you raise in your elaboration.

How do I avoid repeating myself?

Remember that although your topic sentences point back to the thesis statement, you need to avoid using the exact same wording in your topic sentences as in your thesis statement.

For instance, if you refer to the "impersonal nature of electronic communication" in your thesis statement, your topic sentence should word this idea differently.

In this case, the phrase "impersonal nature of electronic communication" could be paraphrased by stating: "There is no direct human contact in email."

Where should a topic sentence be placed within the paragraph?

The most common position for the topic sentence is the first sentence of the paragraph.

In longer essays, it is possible to put a topic sentence as the second sentence of a paragraph if the paragraph's first sentence is transitional.

You can also delay the topic sentence until the end of the paragraph for emphasis, although for the sake of clarity, this is not recommended.

For the Writeplacer essay, you should plan to write two or three main body paragraphs, each of which have a topic sentence as their first sentence.

Topic Sentences – Exercise 1

Let's look again at our sample essay on the suffering of others:

Passage – "Three passions, simple but overwhelmingly strong, have governed my life: the longing for love, the search for knowledge, and unbearable pity for the suffering of mankind." Bertrand Russell

Assignment – Is it ever socially acceptable to be pleased when others suffer?

Suggested introduction:

While feeling pleasure when others suffer is a human emotion to which most of us would not be so quick to admit, there are occasions when it is socially acceptable to take pleasure in the pain of others. Consider, for example, the gratification that the people of European countries would have experienced when Hitler was defeated during the Second World War. Punishment for crime is another occasion where it is not considered untoward to experience satisfaction over the suffering of others. That is to say, although being pleased to see others stricken is normally not acceptable in a civilized society, there are exceptions to this general rule when others have broken the society's norms during times of war or when a criminal is to be punished for his or her wrongdoing.

Your topic sentence for your first body paragraph will mention when others have broken society's norms during times of war.

Your topic sentence for the second body paragraph will mention how a community establishes guidelines for punishing criminals.

Exercise – Now try to write topic sentences for each of your main body paragraphs. Remember that the topic sentence needs to be specific for each supporting point, but general enough to introduce the paragraph as a whole. You may wish to refer back to what you have written thus far on the essay topic. Sample responses are on the next page.

Topic Sentence 1:

Topic Sentence 2:

Topic Sentences – Answer to Exercise 1

Remember that your topic sentence for the first body paragraph should mention when others have broken society's norms during times of war.

The topic sentence for your second body paragraph should mention how a community establishes guidelines for punishing criminals.

You need to re-word the phrases "broken the society's norms during times of war" and "when a criminal is to be punished for his or her wrongdoing" because you have used this exact wording in your thesis statement.

Also bear in mind that you need to connect the viewpoints you express in your topic sentences to the idea that "being pleased to see others stricken is normally not acceptable in a civilized society."

Here are possible topic sentences for your two main body paragraphs.

Topic Sentence 1:

Unfortunately, in modern times we have all too often seen dictators or other despotic rulers who treat the members of their societies harshly, and in such situations, the reactions of those subjected to these regimes is certainly socially justifiable.

Analysis:

The phrase "broken the society's norms during times of war" from the thesis statement has been re-worded and elaborated on by using the phrase "dictators or other despotic rulers who treat the members of their societies harshly."

Topic Sentence 2:

The notion that the punishment should fit the crime is another instance of the acceptability of taking pleasure in someone else's suffering.

Analysis:

The phrase "when a criminal is to be punished for his or her wrongdoing" from the thesis statement is stated as "the punishment should fit the crime" in topic sentence 2.

The phrase "another instance of the acceptability of taking pleasure in someone else's suffering" links the two topic sentences back to the notion that "being pleased to see others stricken is normally not acceptable in a civilized society" from the thesis statement.

Paraphrasing in this way gives your essay coherence and cohesion since it links your ideas together and improves the flow of your writing.

Topic Sentences – Exercise 2

Let's look again at our sample essay on email and text communication:

Most Americans have access to computers and cell phones on a daily basis, making email and text messaging extremely popular. While some people argue that email and texting are now the most convenient forms of personal communication, others believe that electronic communication technology is often used inappropriately. Write an essay for an audience of educated adults in which you take a position on this topic. Be sure to provide reasons and examples to support your viewpoint.

Suggested introduction:

There is no disputing the fact that email and SMS technologies have made our lives easier in a variety of ways. Nevertheless, many of us will have had the experience of falling out with a friend or loved one over an email or text message whose content was poorly written or misconstrued. Clearly, there are certain drawbacks to emails and texts since electronic messaging cannot capture the nuances and subtleties of verbal communication. Modern forms of communication such as electronic mail and SMS messaging can cause problems with personal relationships because of three main shortcomings with these media: their impersonal nature, their inability to capture tone and sarcasm, and their easy accessibility at times of anger.

The topic sentence for your first body paragraph will mention the impersonal nature of electronic communication.

Your topic sentence for the second body paragraph will mention how the tone of emails and texts can be misunderstood.

The topic sentence of your third paragraph will talk about the danger of having a quick messaging service at hand when you are angry.

Exercise – Now try to write topic sentence for each of your main body paragraphs. Remember that the topic sentence needs to be specific for each supporting point, but general enough to introduce the paragraph as a whole. You may wish to refer back to what you have written thus far on the essay topic. Sample responses are on the next page.

Topic Sentence 1:

Topic Sentence 2:

Topic Sentence 3:

Topic Sentences – Answer to Exercise 2

You will recall that our thesis statement was as follows:

> Modern forms of communication such as electronic mail and SMS messaging can cause problems with personal relationships because of three main shortcomings with these media: their impersonal nature, their inability to capture tone and sarcasm, and their easy accessibility at times of anger.

Here are possible topic sentences for the three main body paragraphs.

Topic Sentence 1:

Depending upon the context, the recipient of an email or text message may consider this mode of communication to be insensitive or uncaring.

Analysis:

The phrase "their impersonal nature" from the thesis statement has been re-worded as "insensitive or uncaring."

Topic Sentence 2:

A further problem with emails and texts is that they do not always accurately express the tone which the writer has intended.

Analysis:

The idea of "their inability to capture tone and sarcasm" from the thesis statement has been paraphrased as "they do not always accurately express the tone which the writer has intended."

Topic Sentence 3:

The danger of having an accessible messaging service readily at hand during times of high emotion is another insidious problem with electronic media.

Analysis:

The phrase "their easy accessibility at times of anger" from the thesis statement has been expressed here as "readily at hand during times of high emotion."

Also note that the words "further" from topic sentence 2 and "another" from topic sentence 3 improve the flow of the essay by signaling that new ideas are being introduced in these paragraphs.

Writing the Conclusion

Conclusions for the Writeplacer can consist of as few as two sentences, provided that the sentences are cohesive, coherent, and well-constructed.

As in other parts of your essay, you will need to reiterate certain concepts in the conclusion, without repeating word for word what you have already written.

In particular, your conclusion should echo your introduction, without copying the exact phrases you have used at the start of your essay or in the body paragraphs.

You will continue to need linking words and phrases in the conclusion in order to give a good flow to your writing.

The final sentence of your conclusion can be used to give advice or to make a prediction about the future. This will give a forward-looking aspect to your essay and will help your writing to end on a strong note.

Writing the Conclusion – Exercise 1

Look at the underlined words from the introduction from essay 1 below. Then look at the sample conclusion and identify the words which paraphrase these concepts.

Then circle the linking words and phrases that are used in the sample conclusion.

Introduction from Essay 1:

While <u>feeling pleasure when others suffer</u> is a <u>human emotion to which most of us would not be so quick to admit</u>, there are occasions when it is socially acceptable to take pleasure in the pain of others. Consider, for example, the gratification that the people of European countries would have experienced when Hitler was defeated during the <u>Second World War. Punishment for crime</u> is another occasion where it is not considered untoward to experience satisfaction over the suffering of others. That is to say, although <u>being pleased to see others stricken is normally not acceptable</u> in a civilized society, there are exceptions to this general rule when others have broken the society's norms during times of war or when a criminal is to be punished for his or her wrongdoing.

Sample Conclusion for Essay 1:

Whereas taking delight in the misfortune of others is a trait that normally would not receive social approbation, the circumstances faced in war and crime fall outside this conventional social restriction. However, it is doubtful that *schadenfreude* will ever be considered a socially desirable quality outside these two situations.

Original wording in the introduction: **Paraphrasing in the conclusion:**

feeling pleasure when others suffer

human emotion to which most of us would
not be so quick to admit

. . . Second World War. Punishment for crime . . .

being pleased to see others stricken is
normally not acceptable

What advice or prediction is made in the conclusion to essay 1?

Writing the Conclusion – Answer to Exercise 1

Introduction from Essay 1:

While <u>feeling pleasure when others suffer</u> is a <u>human emotion to which most of us would not be so quick to admit</u>, there are occasions when it is socially acceptable to take pleasure in the pain of others. Consider, for example, the gratification that the people of European countries would have experienced when Hitler was defeated during the <u>Second World War. Punishment for crime</u> is another occasion where it is not considered untoward to experience satisfaction over the suffering of others. That is to say, although <u>being pleased to see others stricken is normally not acceptable</u> in a civilized society, there are exceptions to this general rule when others have broken the society's norms during times of war or when a criminal is to be punished for his or her wrongdoing.

Conclusion for Essay 1:

Whereas taking delight in the misfortune of others is a trait that normally would not receive social approbation, the circumstances faced in war and crime fall outside this conventional social restriction. However, it is doubtful that *schadenfreude* will ever be considered a socially desirable quality outside these two situations.

Original wording in the introduction:	Paraphrasing in the conclusion:
feeling pleasure when others suffer	taking delight in the misfortune of others
human emotion to which most of us would not be so quick to admit	a trait that normally would not receive social approbation
. . . Second World War. Punishment for crime . . .	war and crime
being pleased to see others stricken is normally not acceptable	fall outside this conventional social restriction

Linking words and phrases in the conclusion:

whereas

however

What advice or prediction is made in the conclusion to essay 1?

The following prediction is stated in the last sentence of the conclusion to essay 1: "It is doubtful that *schadenfreude* will ever be considered a socially desirable quality outside these two situations."

Writing the Conclusion – Exercise 2

Look at the underlined words from the introduction from essay 2 below. Then look at the sample conclusion and identify the words which paraphrase these concepts.

Then circle the linking words and phrases that are used in the sample conclusion.

Introduction from Essay 2:

There is no disputing the fact that <u>email and SMS technologies have made our lives easier in a variety of ways</u>. Nevertheless, many of us will have had the experience of falling out with a friend or loved one over an email or text message whose content was poorly written or misconstrued. Clearly, <u>there are certain drawbacks to emails and texts</u> since electronic messaging <u>cannot capture the nuances</u> and <u>subtleties of verbal communication</u>. Modern forms of communication such as electronic mail and SMS messaging can cause problems with personal relationships because of three main shortcomings with these media: their impersonal nature, their inability to capture tone and sarcasm, and their easy accessibility at times of anger.

Conclusion for Essay 2:

While email and texts may therefore be useful for certain aspects of our daily lives, these communication methods need to be handled with care in some situations, particularly when they could be seen as insensitive, when it is possible that the recipient might misinterpret the meaning, or when composed at times of personal agitation or stress. The writer of the message should use judgment and common sense in order to avoid the ill feelings that may be caused to the recipient in these cases.

Original wording in the introduction:

email and SMS technologies have made our lives easier in a variety of ways

there are certain drawbacks to emails and texts

cannot capture the nuances

subtleties of verbal communication

Paraphrasing in the conclusion:

Linking words and phrases in the conclusion:

What advice or prediction is made in the conclusion to essay 2?

Writing the Conclusion – Answer to Exercise 2

Introduction from Essay 2:

There is no disputing the fact that <u>email and SMS technologies have made our lives easier in a variety of ways</u>. Nevertheless, many of us will have had the experience of falling out with a friend or loved one over an email or text message whose content was poorly written or misconstrued. Clearly, <u>there are certain drawbacks to emails and texts</u> since electronic messaging <u>cannot capture the nuances</u> and <u>subtleties of verbal communication</u>. Modern forms of communication such as electronic mail and SMS messaging can cause problems with personal relationships because of three main shortcomings with these media: their impersonal nature, their inability to capture tone and sarcasm, and their easy accessibility at times of anger.

Conclusion for Essay 2:

While email and texts may therefore be useful for certain aspects of our daily lives, these communication methods need to be handled with care in some situations, particularly when they could be seen as insensitive, when it is possible that the recipient might misinterpret the meaning, or when composed at times of personal agitation or stress. The writer of the message should use judgment and common sense in order to avoid the ill feelings that may be caused to the recipient in these cases.

Original wording in the introduction:	**Paraphrasing in the conclusion:**
email and SMS technologies have made our lives easier in a variety of ways	email and texts may therefore be useful for certain aspects of our daily lives
there are certain drawbacks to emails and texts	these communication methods need to be handled with care in some situations
cannot capture the nuances	could be seen as insensitive . . .
subtleties of verbal communication	the recipient might misinterpret the meaning

Linking words and phrases in the conclusion:

while

particularly

when

in order to

What advice or prediction is made in the conclusion to essay 2?

The following piece of advice is given in the last sentence of the conclusion to essay 2: The writer of the message should use judgment and common sense in order to avoid the ill feelings that may be caused to the recipient in these cases.

Using Correct Grammar and Punctuation

Mechanical conventions are the rules of grammar and punctuation that are necessary in order to write accurately and correctly.

This section is intended as a basic overview of some of the most important mechanical conventions for the Writeplacer exam.

Comparatives and Superlatives – Avoid Using Double Forms:

Use the comparative form when comparing two things.

The comparative form consists of the adjective plus –er when the adjective has two syllables or less.

pretty → prettier

Avoid making a double comparative:

INCORRECT: more prettier

When the adjective has more than two syllables, the adjective should be preceded by the word "more" in order to form the comparative.

beautiful → more beautiful

Examples:

Tom is taller than his brother.

Tom is more intelligent than his brother.

If you are comparing more than two things, you must use the superlative form.

As a general rule, the superlative form consists of the adjective plus –est when the adjective has two syllables or less.

pretty → prettiest

Avoid making a double superlative:

INCORRECT: most prettiest

To form the superlative for adjectives that have more than two syllables, the adjective should be preceded by the word "most".

beautiful → most beautiful

Examples:

Tom is the tallest boy in his class.

Tom is the most intelligent boy in his class.

Correct Use of *Its* and *It's*:

"Its" is a possessive pronoun, while "it's" is a contraction of "it is."

CORRECT: It's high time you started to study.

INCORRECT: Its high time you started to study.

The sentence could also be stated as follows: It is high time that you started to study.

Since the contracted form of "it is" is used in the alternative sentence, "it's" is the correct form.

CORRECT: A snake sheds its skin at least once a year.

INCORRECT: A snake sheds it's skin at least once a year.

"Its" is a possessive pronoun referring to the snake, so the apostrophe should not be used.

Correct Use of *Their*, *There*, and *They're*:

"Their" is a plural possessive pronoun.

"There" is used to describe the location of something.

"They're" is a contraction of "they are."

CORRECT: Their house is made of brick and concrete.

INCORRECT: There house is made of brick and concrete.

INCORRECT: They're house is made of brick and concrete.

In this case, "their" is the possessive pronoun explaining to whom the house belongs.

CORRECT: He attended college with his cousins living there in California.

INCORRECT: He attended college with his cousins living their in California.

INCORRECT: He attended college with his cousins living they're in California.

"There" is referring to the state of California in the example above, so it is used to talk about the location.

CORRECT: They're away on vacation at the moment.

INCORRECT: Their away on vacation at the moment.

INCORRECT: There away on vacation at the moment.

The sentence could also be written as follows: They are away on vacation at the moment.

"They're" is a contraction of "they are," so the apostrophe needs to be used.

Correct Use of *Were*, *Where*, and *We're*:

"Were" is the past tense of the verb "are."

"Where" is used to inquire about or describe the location of something.

"We're" is a contraction of "we are."

CORRECT: They were going to call you, but the phone was out of order.

INCORRECT: They where going to call you, but the phone was out of order.

INCORRECT: They we're going to call you, but the phone was out of order.

"Were" is the past form of the verb in the sentence above.

CORRECT: Where is the mall located?

INCORRECT: Were is the mall located?

INCORRECT: We're is the mall located?

"Where" needs to be used because the sentence is making an inquiry about the location of the mall.

CORRECT: We're so happy that you got accepted into college.

INCORRECT: Were so happy that you got accepted into college.

INCORRECT: Where so happy that you got accepted into college.

The sentence could be written as follows: We are so happy that you got accepted into college.

"We're" is a contraction of "we are," so the apostrophe needs to be used.

Avoid the "is where" construction:

CORRECT: An identity crisis, which is the experience of confusion about one's life goals and ambitions, often occurs in middle age.

INCORRECT: An identity crisis is where there is the experience of confusion about one's life goals and ambitions, and it often occurs in middle age.

The construction in the second sentence may be used in informal speaking, but such constructions should be avoided in your essay.

Misplaced Modifiers:

Modifiers are phrases that describe other parts of a sentence. The modifier should always be placed directly before or after the noun to which it relates.

Now look at these examples:

CORRECT: Like Minnesota, Wisconsin gets extremely cold in the winter.

INCORRECT: Like Minnesota, it gets extremely cold in Wisconsin in the winter.

The phrase "like Minnesota" is an adjectival phrase that modifies the noun "Wisconsin."

Therefore, "Wisconsin" must come directly after the comma.

Here are two more examples:

CORRECT: While at the mall, a gang of youths committed a robbery.

INCORRECT: While at the mall, a robbery was committed.

The adverbial phrase "while at the mall" modifies the noun phrase "a gang of youths," so this noun phrase needs to come after the adverbial phrase.

Parallelism:

When giving items in a series, be sure to use consistent forms.

CORRECT: The position involves answering phone calls, writing letters, and getting supplies.

INCORRECT: The position involves answering phone calls, writing letters, and get supplies.

All of the items in the series should be in the –ing form.

CORRECT: I saw Tom's accident yesterday, and I tried to help.

INCORRECT: I saw Tom's accident yesterday, and I try to help.

Both parts of the sentence are describing actions that occurred yesterday, so the past tense (–ed) needs to be used for both verbs.

Punctuation and Independent Clauses – Avoiding Run-On Sentences:

Run-on sentences are those that use commas to join independent clauses together, instead of correctly using the period.

An independent clause contains a grammatical subject and verb. It therefore can stand alone as its own sentence.

The first word of the independent clause should begin with a capital letter, and the clause should be preceded by a period.

CORRECT: I thought I would live in this city forever. Then I lost my job.

INCORRECT: I thought I would live in this city forever, then I lost my job.

"Then I lost my job" is a complete sentence. It has a grammatical subject (I) and a verb (lost). The independent clause must be preceded by a period, and the first word of the new sentence must begin with a capital letter.

Alternatively, an appropriate conjunction can be used to join the independent clauses:

I thought I would live in this city forever, and then I lost my job.

Punctuation and Quotation Marks:

Punctuation should be enclosed within the final quotation mark when giving dialogue.

CORRECT: "I can't believe you bought a new car," Sam remarked.

INCORRECT: "I can't believe you bought a new car", Sam remarked.

In the example below, the word "exclaimed" shows that the exclamation point is needed.

CORRECT: "I can't believe you bought a new car!" Sam exclaimed.

INCORRECT: "I can't believe you bought a new car"! Sam exclaimed. However, if the quotation is stated indirectly, no quotation marks should be used.

CORRECT: Sam exclaimed that he couldn't believe that I had bought a new car.

INCORRECT: Sam exclaimed that "he couldn't believe that I had bought a new car."

Punctuation for Items in a Series:

When using "and" and "or" for more than two items in a series, be sure to use the comma before the words "and" and "or."

CORRECT: You need to bring a tent, sleeping bag, and flashlight.

INCORRECT: You need to bring a tent, sleeping bag and flashlight.

Notice the use of the comma after the word "bag" and before the word "and" in the series.

CORRECT: Students can call, write a letter, or send an email.

INCORRECT: Students can call, write a letter or send an email.

Notice the use of the comma after the word "letter" and before the word "or" in the series.

Restrictive and Non-restrictive Modifiers:

Restrictive modifiers are clauses or phrases that provide essential information in order to identify the grammatical subject. Restrictive modifiers should not be preceded by a comma.

Example: My sister who lives in Indianapolis is a good swimmer.

In this case, the speaker has more than one sister, and she is identifying which sister she is talking about by giving the essential information "who lives in Indianapolis."

On the other hand, a non-restrictive modifier is a clause or phrase that provides extra information about a grammatical subject in a sentence. A non-restrictive modifier must be preceded by a comma.

Non-restrictive modifiers are also known as non-essential modifiers.

Example: My sister, who lives in Indianapolis, is a good swimmer.

In this case, the speaker has only one sister. Therefore, the information about her sister's city of residence is not essential in order to identify which sister she is talking about.

The words "who lives in Indianapolis" form a non-restrictive modifier.

Sentence Fragments:

A sentence fragment is a group of words that does not express a complete train of thought.

CORRECT: I like Denver because it has a great university.

INCORRECT: I like Denver. Because it has a great university.

In the second example, "because it has a great university" is not a complete thought. This idea needs to be joined with the previous clause in order to be grammatically correct.

Subject-Verb Agreement:

Subjects must agree with verbs in number.

Subject-verb agreement can be confusing when there are intervening words in a sentence.

CORRECT: The flowers in the pots in the garden grow quickly.

INCORRECT: The flowers in the pots in the garden grows quickly.

The grammatical subject in the above sentence is "flowers," not "garden," so the plural form of the verb (*grow*) needs to be used.

CORRECT: Each person in the groups of students needs to pay attention to the instructions.

INCORRECT: Each person in the groups of students need to pay attention to the instructions.

The grammatical subject in the above sentence is "each person," not "students." "Each" is singular and therefore needs the singular form of the verb (*needs*).

Using Correct Grammar and Punctuation – Exercises

Each of the sentences below has problems with grammar and punctuation. Find the errors in the sentences and correct them. You may wish to refer to the advice in the previous section as you do the exercise.

The answers are provided on the page following the exercises.

1) I haven't seen her or her sister. Since they went away to college.

2) People who like to get up early in the morning in order to drink more coffee is likely to become easily tired in the afternoon.

3) Were we're you when we called you yesterday?

4) She is the most happiest person that I know.

5) Hanging from the knob on the bedroom door, Tom thought the new shirt was his favorite.

6) I ran across the street to speak to her, then she surprised me by saying "that she had bought a new car."

7) Its common for a magazine to have better sales if it mentions computers, handhelds or other new technology on it's cover.

8) After losing long-term employment, many people suffer from anxiety, loneliness and get depressed.

9) Each student in the class who will take the series of exams on advanced mathematics need to study in advance.

10) Their are several reasons why there having problems with they're children.

Using Correct Grammar and Punctuation – Answers

1) I haven't seen her or her sister since they went away to college.

2) People who like to get up early in the morning in order to drink more coffee are likely to become easily tired in the afternoon.

3) Where were you when we called you yesterday?

4) She is the happiest person that I know.

5) Hanging from the knob on the bedroom door, the new shirt was Tom's favorite.

6) I ran across the street to speak to her. Then she surprised me by saying that she had bought a new car.

7) It's common for a magazine to have better sales if it mentions computers, handhelds, or other new technology on its cover.

8) After losing long-term employment, many people suffer from anxiety, loneliness, and depression.

9) Each student in the class who will take the series of exams on advanced mathematics needs to study in advance.

10) There are several reasons why they're having problems with their children.

The Importance of Vocabulary for the Writeplacer – Using the Academic Word List

As mentioned at the beginning of this study guide, the Writeplacer uses automated scoring software.

This means that you will receive the score for your essay on the computer screen within moments of clicking the "submit" button.

This study guide has covered the various aspects of grammar and structure that you need to demonstrate in your essay.

However, the scoring software also assesses your vocabulary level as it moves through the various paragraphs of your essay.

The following pages contain a list of academic words. You should study the list and try to use these words in your Writeplacer essay.

An exercise on academic vocabulary follows the two sample essays.

Academic Word List

abundant	aspect
acceptability	atrocity
acceptable	attribute
access	believe
accessibility	capacity
accessible	catalyst
accumulate	category
accurate	caveat
acknowledge	circumstance
acquire	cite
admit	claim
adversity	clarify
advocate	codify
affirm	coherent
aggregate	comment
agitate	communicate
agitation	compile
analogy	compose
announce	comprehensive
approbation	conclude
appropriate	concurrent
approve	conduct
arguably	confirm
argue	consider

consist

constitute

construct

consult

contemplate

contradict

contravene

controversy

convenient

convention

conventional

convey

create

credence

criteria

crucial

decline

deduce

demonstrate

deny

despotic

determine

deterrent

derive

deviate

differentiate

diminish

discern

discipline

discriminate

dispose

dispute

distribute

diverse

document

dominate

drawback

eliminate

emerge

emphasize

empirical

encounter

enforce

enhance

enumerate

environment

equate

equivalent

erode

establish

estimate	heinous
evaluate	hierarchy
evident	highlight
exhibit	hypothesis
exist	identify
existence	ideology
experience	illustrate
explicit	immense
exploit	impact
extract	implement
facilitate	implicate
factor	imply
feature	inappropriate
fluctuate	incentive
focus	incidence
formula	indicate
foundation	individual
framework	induce
fundamental	inevitable
general	infer
generate	inflection
grant	inhabitant
gratification	inherent
gratify	innovate
guideline	input

insidious	liberal
insight	literal
inspect	locate
instance	logic
instruct	maintain
integral	major
integrity	manipulate
intense	maximize
interact	mechanism
interpret	media
intervene	mediate
intrinsic	method
investigate	minimize
invoke	misconstrue
involve	misfortune
ironically	misinterpret
irretrievable	mode
isolate	modify
issue	motive
item	mutual
judgment	negate
justify	network
labor	neutral
legislate	norm
levy	notion

nuance

objective

observe

obtain

occasion

occupy

occur

offender

offset

ongoing

option

outcome

oversee

paradigm

parallel

parameter

participate

perceive

persecute

perspective

phenomenon

philosophy

policy

possession

postulate

potential

precede

precise

predict

predominant

preliminary

presume

previous

primary

principal

priority

process

professional

prohibit

promote

proportion

propose

prospect

protocol

publication

purchase

pursue

quote

rational

recipient

recover	revenue
refine	reverse
refute	revise
regime	satisfaction
register	satisfy
regrettable	scenario
regulate	schadenfreude
reinforce	scheme
reject	scope
release	select
relevant	sequence
reluctant	shortcoming
remarkable	significant
repudiate	situation
require	specific
research	specify
reside	statistic
resolve	status
resource	stipulate
respond	straightforward
restore	strategy
restrain	stricken
restrict	structure
restriction	submit
reveal	subordinate

subsequent

subtlety

sufficient

summary

supplement

surrender

survey

suspend

sustain

technique

technology

terminate

theory

transform

ultimate

ultimatum

undergo

underlie

undertake

unfortunate

uniform

unimaginable

unique

unthinkable

untoward

utilize

utter

utterance

valid

vary

version

widespread

would-be

wrongdoing

Sample Essay 1

Below we reproduce in full sample essays 1 and 2, which we have worked on throughout the various sections of this study guide. Look at each essay below. Then identify the academic vocabulary in each one. Note that the forms used in the essay may differ slightly from those provided in the academic word list in the previous section. You may need to find plural forms or past tense, for example. The answers for both exercises are provided after sample essay 2.

Essay 1:

While feeling pleasure when others suffer is a human emotion to which most of us would not be so quick to admit, there are occasions when it is socially acceptable to take pleasure in the pain of others. Consider, for example, the gratification that the people of European countries would have experienced when Hitler was defeated during the Second World War. Punishment for crime is another occasion where it is not considered untoward to experience satisfaction over the suffering of others. That is to say, although being pleased to see others stricken is normally not acceptable in a civilized society, there are exceptions to this general rule when others have broken the society's norms during times of war or when a criminal is to be punished for his or her wrongdoing.

Unfortunately, in modern times we have all too often seen dictators or other despotic rulers who treat the members of their societies harshly, and in such situations, the reactions of those subjected to these regimes is certainly socially justifiable. Adolph Hitler, arguably the most notorious dictator of the twentieth century, committed countless heinous acts against the inhabitants of several European countries during World War II. Due to his atrocities, previously contented residents of many towns and villages had to flee their homes in fear, leaving behind all of their worldly possessions. The most unfortunate of these persecuted individuals were submitted to unthinkable states of existence in the many death camps that Hitler oversaw. Because they were forced to live in such unimaginable conditions, those that Hitler persecuted must have been gratified when the dictator faced adversity during the war. Once Hitler had encountered the final ultimatum of surrender or death and his regime was overthrown, the relief and satisfaction openly expressed around the world on a personal level was immense.

The notion that the punishment should fit the crime is another instance of the acceptability of taking pleasure in another's suffering. Criminal law, which has been created according to traditional social convention, has been established to ensure that offenders will be justly tried and punished for their crimes. When someone has broken the norms of society in this way, other members of the community feel satisfied because they believe that justice has been served when the offender has been punished. In addition, punishing social wrongs can act as a deterrent to would-be criminals, thereby further reinforcing social norms.

Whereas taking delight in the misfortune of others is a trait that normally would not receive social approbation, the circumstances faced in war and crime fall outside this conventional social restriction. However, it is doubtful that *schadenfreude* will ever be considered a socially desirable quality outside these two situations.

Sample Essay 2

Essay 2:

There is no disputing the fact that email and SMS technologies have made our lives easier in a variety of ways. Nevertheless, many of us will have had the experience of falling out with a friend or loved one over an email or text message whose content was poorly written or misconstrued. Clearly, there are certain drawbacks to emails and texts since electronic messaging cannot capture the nuances and subtleties of verbal communication. Modern forms of communication such as electronic mail and SMS messaging can cause problems with personal relationships because of three main shortcomings with these media: their impersonal nature, their inability to capture tone and sarcasm, and their easy accessibility at times of anger.

Depending upon the context, the recipient of an email or text message may consider this mode of communication to be insensitive or uncaring. Although email may be practical for conveying straightforward information or facts, electronic messaging would be remarkably inappropriate for events like announcing a death. There is no direct human contact in emails and texts, and during times of loss or tragedy, human warmth and depth of emotion can only truly be conveyed through a phone call, or better still, by talking face to face.

A further problem with emails and texts is that they do not always accurately express the tone which the writer has intended. For instance, it might be possible for the recipient of a sarcastic email message to take its contents literally. The tone of the message may seem abundantly clear to the person who sent it, but sarcastic or ironically humorous utterances can only really be communicated in speech through the tone and inflection of the voice. Without the aid of tone and inflection, certain phrases in an email may come across as demanding, indifferent, or rude.

The danger of having an accessible messaging service readily at hand during times of high emotion is another insidious problem with electronic media. In this day and age, we have heard stories not only of personal break ups that have been conducted by text, but also of employers who fire their staff by email message. Unless the writer of the message has the discipline and self-control to give him or herself a period of reasoned contemplation before sending the communication, he or she might send a regrettable message that can cause irretrievable damage to a relationship.

While email and texts may therefore be useful for certain aspects of our daily lives, these communication methods need to be handled with care in some situations, particularly when they could be seen as insensitive, when it is possible that the recipient might misinterpret the meaning, or when composed at times of personal agitation or stress. The writer of the message should use judgment and common sense in order to avoid the ill feelings that may be caused to the recipient in these cases.

Sample Essay 1 – Answers

Here is a list of the academic vocabulary used in sample essay 1:

admit	submit
occasions	unthinkable
acceptable	existence
gratify	oversaw
gratification	unimaginable
experienced	persecuted
untoward	adversity
satisfaction	encountered
stricken	ultimatum
general	surrender
norms	immense
wrongdoing	notion
despotic	instance
regime	acceptability
justifiable	created
arguably	conventions
heinous	established
inhabitant	offenders
atrocities	norms
possession	deterrent
unfortunate	would-be
individual	misfortune

approbation	restriction
circumstances	schadenfreude
conventional	situations

Sample Essay 2 – Answers

Here is a list of the academic vocabulary used in sample essay 2:

disputing	conducted
misconstrued	discipline
drawbacks	contemplation
nuances	regrettable
subtleties	irretrievable
shortcomings	aspects
media	recipient
accessibility	misinterpret
consider	composed
conveying	agitation
straightforward	judgment
remarkably	
announcing	
accurately	
recipient	
literally	
abundantly	
ironically	
utterance	
inflection	
accessible	
insidious	

ADVANTAGE+ EDITION – BONUS MATERIAL

ESSAY CORRECTION EXERCISES

Instructions: The draft essays below contain errors. Choose the correct version of each part of each sentence from the answer choices provided. If the part of the sentence is correct as written, you should choose answer A. The answers are provided at the end of the exercises.

Essay 1 – Antarctica

[1] Antarctica is a mysterious and resilient continent [2] one which is often forgotten by virtue of its geographical location. [3] Now that the Antarctic is remote and desolate. [4] Nevertheless, an understanding of the organisms that inhabit this continent was critical [5] to our comprehension of the world as a global community. [6] For this reason, the southernmost continent has the source of a great deal of scientific investigation.

[7] Many notable recent research has come from America and Great Britain. [8] The British Antarctic Survey, sponsored with the Natural Environment Research Council of the United Kingdom, [9] and the United States Antarctic Resource Center, a collaborate of the United States Geological Survey Mapping Division and the National Science Foundation, [10] are forerunners in the burgeoning currently field of research in this area.

[11] This corpus of research has resulted in an abundance of factual data on the Antarctic. [12] For example, one now know that more than ninety nine percent of the land is completely covered by snow and ice, [13] which making Antarctica the coldest continent on the planet. [14] This inhospitable climate, has not surprisingly, brought about the adaptation [15] of a plethora of plants and biological organisms on the continent present. [16] An investigation for the sedimentary geological formations provides testimony to the process of adaptation. [17] Ancient

sediment's recovered from the bottom of Antarctic lakes, [18] bacteria as well as discovered in ice, [19] has reveal the history of climate change over the past 10,000 years.

Item 1.
- A. Antarctica is a mysterious and resilient continent
- B. Antarctica is a mysterious and resounding continent
- C. Antarctica is a mysterious and respectable continent
- D. Antarctica is a mysterious and resistant continent
- E. Antarctica is a mysterious and restrained continent

Item 2.
- A. one which is often forgotten by virtue of its geographical location.
- B. one whose often forgotten by virtue of its geographical location.
- C. that is often forgotten by virtue of its geographical location.
- D. this is often forgotten by virtue of its geographical location.
- E. those are often forgotten by virtue of its geographical location.

Item 3.
- A. Now that the Antarctic is remote and desolate.
- B. Always, the Antarctic is remote and desolate.
- C. Since the Antarctic is remote and desolate.
- D. Indeed, the Antarctic is remote and desolate.
- E. On the other hand, the Antarctic is remote and desolate.

Item 4.
- A. Nevertheless, an understanding of the organisms that inhabit this continent was critical
- B. Nevertheless, an understanding of the organisms that inhabit this continent were critical
- C. Nevertheless, an understanding of the organisms that inhabit this continent is critical
- D. Nevertheless, an understanding of the organisms that inhabit this continent are critical
- E. Nevertheless, an understanding of the organisms that inhabit this continent are being critical

Item 5.
- A. to our comprehension of the world as a global community.
- B. to our comprehension at the world as a global community.
- C. to our comprehension in the world as a global community.
- D. to our comprehension about the world as a global community.
- E. to our comprehension for the world as a global community.

Item 6.
- A. For this reason, the southernmost continent has the source of a great deal of scientific investigation.
- B. For this reason, the southernmost continent has been the source of a great deal of scientific investigation.
- C. For this reason, the southernmost continent was the source of a great deal of scientific investigation.
- D. For this reason, the southernmost continent has to be the source of a great deal of scientific investigation.
- E. For this reason, the southernmost continent had the source of a great deal of scientific investigation.

Item 7.
- A. Many notable recent research has come from America and Great Britain.
- B. Much notable recent research has come from America and Great Britain.
- C. More notable recent research has come from America and Great Britain.
- D. More than notable recent research has come from America and Great Britain.
- E. As much as notable recent research has come from America and Great Britain.

Item 8.
- A. The British Antarctic Survey, sponsored with the Natural Environment Research Council of the United Kingdom,
- B. The British Antarctic Survey, sponsored by the Natural Environment Research Council of the United Kingdom,
- C. The British Antarctic Survey, sponsored against the Natural Environment Research Council of the United Kingdom,

D. The British Antarctic Survey, sponsored from the Natural Environment Research Council of the United Kingdom,

E. The British Antarctic Survey, sponsored upon the Natural Environment Research Council of the United Kingdom,

Item 9.

A. and the United States Antarctic Resource Center, a collaborate of the United States Geological Survey Mapping Division and the National Science Foundation,

B. And the United States Antarctic Resource Center, a collaborative of the United States Geological Survey Mapping Division and the National Science Foundation,

C. and the United States Antarctic Resource Center, a collaboratively of the United States Geological Survey Mapping Division and the National Science Foundation,

D. and the United States Antarctic Resource Center, a collaboration of the United States Geological Survey Mapping Division and the National Science Foundation,

E. and the United States Antarctic Resource Center, a collaborator of the United States Geological Survey Mapping Division and the National Science Foundation,

Item 10.

A. are forerunners in the burgeoning currently field of research in this area.
B. are forerunners in the burgeoning field of currently research in this area.
C. are currently forerunners in the burgeoning field of research in this area.
D. are forerunners in the burgeoning field of research in currently this area.
E. are forerunners in the burgeoning field of research in this currently area.

Item 11.

A. This corpus of research has resulted in an abundance of factual data on the Antarctic.
B. This corpus of research was resulted in an abundance of factual data on the Antarctic.
C. This corpus of research has been resulted in an abundance of factual data on the Antarctic.
D. This corpus of research was resulting in an abundance of factual data on the Antarctic.
E. This corpus of research resulting in an abundance of factual data on the Antarctic.

Item 12.
- A. For example, one now know that more than ninety nine percent of the land is completely covered by snow and ice,
- B. For example, we now know that more than ninety nine percent of the land is completely covered by snow and ice,
- C. For example, they now knows that more than ninety nine percent of the land is completely covered by snow and ice,
- D. For example, the community now know that more than ninety nine percent of the land is completely covered by snow and ice,
- E. For example, the research now know that more than ninety nine percent of the land is completely covered by snow and ice,

Item 13.
- A. which making Antarctica the coldest continent on the planet.
- B. which is making Antarctica the coldest continent on the planet.
- C. making Antarctica the coldest continent on the planet.
- D. has made Antarctica the coldest continent on the planet.
- E. that made Antarctica the coldest continent on the planet.

Item 14.
- A. This inhospitable climate, has not surprisingly, brought about the adaptation
- B. This inhospitable climate has, not surprisingly, brought about the adaptation
- C. This inhospitable climate has, not surprisingly; brought about the adaptation
- D. This inhospitable climate has not surprisingly: brought about the adaptation
- E. This inhospitable climate has not surprisingly, brought about the adaptation

Item 15.
- A. of a plethora of plants and biological organisms on the continent present.
- B. of a plethora of plants and biological organisms present on the continent.
- C. of a plethora on the continent of plants and biological organisms present.
- D. of a plethora of plants on the continent and biological organisms present.
- E. of a plethora of plants and on the continent biological organisms present.

Item 16.
- A. An investigation for the sedimentary geological formations provides testimony to the process of adaptation.
- B. An investigation within the sedimentary geological formations provides testimony to the process of adaptation.
- C. An investigation at the sedimentary geological formations provides testimony to the process of adaptation.
- D. An investigation about the sedimentary geological formations provides testimony to the process of adaptation.
- E. An investigation into the sedimentary geological formations provides testimony to the process of adaptation.

Item 17.
- A. Ancient sediment's recovered from the bottom of Antarctic lakes,
- B. Ancient sediments' recovered from the bottom of Antarctic lakes,
- C. Ancient sediments recovered from the bottom of Antarctic lakes,
- D. Ancient's sediment recovered from the bottom of Antarctic lakes,
- E. Ancient's sediments recovered from the bottom of Antarctic lakes,

Item 18.
- A. bacteria as well as discovered in ice,
- B. as well as bacteria discovered in ice,
- C. bacteria discovered as well as in ice,
- D. bacteria discovered in as well as ice,
- E. bacteria discovered in ice as well,

Item 19.
- A. has reveal the history of climate change over the past 10,000 years.
- B. has revealed the history of climate change over the past 10,000 years.
- C. have reveal the history of climate change over the past 10,000 years.
- D. have revealed the history of climate change over the past 10,000 years.
- E. have been revealed the history of climate change over the past 10,000 years.

Item 20.

If the student were to add a paragraph at the end of the essay explaining that the reliability of the research on Antarctica has been disputed, the essay would lose:

    A.   its academic tone.

    B.   its clarity and focus.

    C.   the sense that this topic of current interest.

    D.   its emphasis on the inhospitality of the Antarctic climate.

    E.   the sense of importance it places on the scientific evidence.

Essay 2 – Population Age-Sex Structure

[1] The major significant characteristic of any population is its age-sex structure, [2] defining as the proportion of people of each gender in each different age group. [3] The age-sex structure determines the potential for reproduction, [4] and for example population growth, [5] based on the balance of males and females of child-bearing age inside a population. [6] Thus, the age-sex structure was social policy implications.

[7] For instance, a population with a high proportion of citizens elderly [8] needs to consider its governmental-funded pension schemes and health care systems carefully. [9] As follows: a demographic with a greater percentage of young children should ensure [10] which its educational funding and child welfare policies are implemented efficaciously. [11] Accordingly, as the composition of a population changes against time, [12] the government may need to restate its funding priorities.

[13] For it is possible that a population may have low birth rates [14] resulting an imbalance in the age-sex structure. [15] Low birth rate's might also be attributable to governmental policy that attempts to control the population. [16] Policies are one example of that restrict the number of children a family can have this outcome. [17] Other possible reason for these types of demographic changes might be unnaturally high death rates, [18] such like in the case of a disease epidemic or natural disaster. [19] Finally, migration is another factor [20] in demographic attrition, because in any population, a certain amount of people, may decide to emigrate, or move to a different country.

Item 1.
- A. The major significant characteristic of any population is its age-sex structure,
- B. The majorly significant characteristic of any population is its age-sex structure,
- C. The most significantly characteristic of any population is its age-sex structure,

- D. The most significant characteristic of any population is its age-sex structure,
- E. The more significant characteristic of any population is its age-sex structure,

Item 2.
- A. defining as the proportion of people of each gender in each different age group.
- B. defined as the proportion of people of each gender in each different age group.
- C. which defining as the proportion of people of each gender in each different age group.
- D. which defined as the proportion of people of each gender in each different age group.
- E. as defined as the proportion of people of each gender in each different age group.

Item 3.
- A. The age-sex structure determines the potential for reproduction,
- B. The age-sex structure determined the potential for reproduction,
- C. The age-sex structure has determined the potential for reproduction,
- D. The age-sex structure had determined the potential for reproduction,
- E. The age-sex structure was determined the potential for reproduction,

Item 4.
- A. and for example population growth,
- B. and so that population growth,
- C. and with regard to population growth,
- D. and it follows that population growth,
- E. and as a consequence population growth,

Item 5.
- A. based on the balance of males and females of child-bearing age inside a population.
- B. based on the balance of males and females of child-bearing age within a population.
- C. based on the balance of males and females of child-bearing age containing a population.
- D. based on the balance of males and females of child-bearing age consisting a population.
- E. based on the balance of males and females of child-bearing age attributing a population.

Item 6.
- A. Thus, the age-sex structure was social policy implications.
- B. Thus, the age-sex structure is social policy implications.
- C. Thus, the age-sex structure has social policy implications.
- D. Thus, the age-sex structure had social policy implications.
- E. Thus, the age-sex structure does social policy implications.

Item 7.
- A. For instance, a population with a high proportion of citizens elderly
- B. For instance, a population with an elderly high proportion of citizens
- C. For instance, a population with a high proportion elderly of citizens
- D. For instance, a population with a high proportion of elderly citizens
- E. For instance, a population with a high elderly proportion of citizens

Item 8.
- A. needs to consider its governmental-funded pension schemes and health care systems carefully.
- B. needs to consider its governmentally-funded pension schemes and health care systems carefully.
- C. needs to consider its funded-governmental pension schemes and health care systems carefully.
- D. needs to consider its funded-governmentally pension schemes and health care systems carefully.
- E. needs to consider its funded governmentally-pension schemes and health care systems carefully.

Item 9.
- A. As follows: a demographic with a greater percentage of young children should ensure
- B. Just as a demographic with a greater percentage of young children should ensure
- C. Conversely, a demographic with a greater percentage of young children should ensure
- D. Despite, a demographic with a greater percentage of young children should ensure
- E. Unless a demographic with a greater percentage of young children should ensure

Item 10.
- A. which its educational funding and child welfare policies are implemented efficaciously.
- B. that its educational funding and child welfare policies are implemented efficaciously.
- C. which it's educational funding and child welfare policies are implemented efficaciously.
- D. that it's educational funding and child welfare policies are implemented efficaciously.
- E. hence its educational funding and child welfare policies are implemented efficaciously.

Item 11.
- A. Accordingly, as the composition of a population changes against time,
- B. Accordingly, as the composition of a population changes for time,
- C. Accordingly, as the composition of a population changes over time,
- D. Accordingly, as the composition of a population changes past time,
- E. Accordingly, as the composition of a population changes as time,

Item 12.
- A. the government may need to restate its funding priorities.
- B. the government may need to re-evaluate its funding priorities.
- C. the government may need to recuperate its funding priorities.
- D. the government may need to cooperate its funding priorities.
- E. the government may need to instigate its funding priorities.

Item 13.
- A. For it is possible that a population may have low birth rates
- B. For this possible that a population may have low birth rates
- C. This is possible that a population may have low birth rates
- D. It is possible that a population may have low birth rates
- E. That is possible that a population may have low birth rates

Item 14.
- A. resulting an imbalance in the age-sex structure.
- B. because an imbalance in the age-sex structure.
- C. due to an imbalance in the age-sex structure.

D. since an imbalance in the age-sex structure.
E. in order to imbalance in the age-sex structure.

Item 15.
A. Low birth rate's might also be attributable to governmental policy that attempts to control the population.
B. Low birth's rates might also be attributable to governmental policy that attempts to control the population.
C. Low births' rates might also be attributable to governmental policy that attempts to control the population.
D. Low birth rates' might also be attributable to governmental policy that attempts to control the population.
E. Low birth rates might also be attributable to governmental policy that attempts to control the population.

Item 16.
A. Policies are one example of that restrict the number of children a family can have this outcome.
B. Policies that restrict are one example of the number of children a family can have this outcome.
C. Policies that restrict the number of children a family can have this outcome are one example.
D. Policies that restrict the number of children a family can have are one example of this outcome.
E. Policies that restrict the number of children a family are one example of this outcome can have.

Item 17.
A. Other possible reason for these types of demographic changes might be unnaturally high death rates,
B. Others possible reason for these types of demographic changes might be unnaturally high death rates,
C. Another possible reason for these types of demographic changes might be unnaturally high death rates,

- D. Anothers possible reason for these types of demographic changes might be unnaturally high death rates,
- E. Another possible reasons for these types of demographic changes might be unnaturally high death rates,

Item 18.
- A. such like in the case of a disease epidemic or natural disaster.
- B. such as in the case of a disease epidemic or natural disaster.
- C. as such as in the case of a disease epidemic or natural disaster.
- D. as its in the case of a disease epidemic or natural disaster.
- E. as much like as in the case of a disease epidemic or natural disaster.

Item 19.
- A. Finally, migration is another factor
- B. Final migration is another factor
- C. Final, migration is another factor
- D. To end, migration is another factor
- E. Conclusively, migration is another factor

Item 20.
- A. in demographic attrition, because in any population, a certain amount of people, may decide to emigrate, or move to a different country.
- B. in demographic attrition because in any population a certain amount of people may decide to emigrate, or move to a different country.
- C. in demographic attrition because, in any population, a certain amount of people may decide to emigrate or move to a different country.
- D. in demographic attrition because in any population, a certain amount of people may decide to emigrate, or move to a different country.
- E. in demographic attrition because in any population a certain amount of people may decide to emigrate or move to a different country.

Item 21.

Suppose that the student was asked to write an essay, the purpose of which was to explain how the government could rectify current deficiencies in the age-sex structure. Has the student achieved this purpose?

- A. Yes, because the student talks about the government's reassessment of funding priorities.
- B. Yes, because the student describes the social policy implication of the age-sex structure.
- C. Yes, because the student explains the effect of governmental policy on low birth rates.
- D. No, because the student fails to provide sufficient examples of the how governmental policy needs to adapt to population changes over time.
- E. No, because the student does not enumerate specific solutions that the government could attempt.

Essay 3 – The Pilgrims

[1] A group of English separatists known as the Pilgrims first left England to live in Amsterdam, in 1608. [2] After spending a few years in their new city, apart from this, many members of the group [3] felt whose they did not have enough independence. [4] Hence, in 1617, the Pilgrims decided to leave Amsterdam immigrating to America.

[5] More of these separatists were poor farmers [6] whom did not have much education or social status, and, not surprisingly, [7] the group had many financial problems that prevented them for beginning their journey. [8] Thereby their inability to finance themselves caused many disputes and disagreements, [9] the Pilgrims finally managing to obtain financing [10] from a well-known and considerable London businessman named Thomas Weston.

[11] Having secured Weston's monetary support, the group returned to England to pick up some additional passengers, [12] and it boarded a large ship called the Mayflower on September 16, 1620. [13] After 65 days at sea, the pilgrim's reached America. [14] Plymouth a town about 35 miles southeast of Boston in the New England state of Massachusetts [15] was established by the Pilgrims in December 21, 1620. [16] Even though the early days of this new lives were filled with hope and promise, [17] the harsh winter proved being too much for some of the settlers. [18] Near half of the Pilgrims died during that first winter, [19] but those who lived go on to work hard and prosper.

Item 1.
- A. A group of English separatists known as the Pilgrims first left England to live in Amsterdam, in 1608.
- B. A group of English separatists known as the Pilgrims first left England to live, in Amsterdam, in 1608.
- C. A group of English separatists known as the Pilgrims first left England to live in Amsterdam in 1608.
- D. A group of English separatists known as the Pilgrims, first left England to live in Amsterdam, in 1608.
- E. A group of English separatists known as the Pilgrims, first left England to live, in Amsterdam in 1608.

Item 2.
- A. After spending a few years in their new city, apart from this, many members of the group
- B. After spending a few years in their new city, in this case, many members of the group
- C. After spending a few years in their new city, namely, many members of the group
- D. After spending a few years in their new city, however, many members of the group
- E. After spending a few years in their new city, otherwise, many members of the group

Item 3.
- A. felt whose they did not have enough independence.
- B. felt whom they did not have enough independence.
- C. felt which they did not have enough independence.
- D. felt that they did not have enough independence.
- E. felt in that they did not have enough independence.

Item 4.
- A. Hence, in 1617, the Pilgrims decided to leave Amsterdam immigrating to America.
- B. Hence, in 1617, the Pilgrims decided to leave Amsterdam to immigrate to America.
- C. Hence, in 1617, the Pilgrims decided to leave Amsterdam emigrating to America.
- D. Hence, in 1617, the Pilgrims decided to leave Amsterdam to emigrate to America.
- E. Hence, in 1617, the Pilgrims decided to leave Amsterdam for migrating to America.

Item 5.
- A. More of these separatists were poor farmers
- B. Much of these separatists were poor farmers
- C. Many of these separatists were poor farmers
- D. Many more of these separatists were poor farmers
- E. The most of these separatists were poor farmers

Item 6.
- A. whom did not have much education or social status, and, not surprisingly,
- B. of whom did not have much education or social status, and, not surprisingly,
- C. whose did not have much education or social status, and, not surprisingly,
- D. which did not have much education or social status, and, not surprisingly,
- E. who did not have much education or social status, and, not surprisingly,

Item 7.
- A. the group had many financial problems that prevented them for beginning their journey.
- B. the group had many financial problems that prevented them to beginning their journey.
- C. the group had many financial problems that prevented them from beginning their journey.
- D. the group had many financial problems that prevented them against beginning their journey.
- E. the group had many financial problems that prevented them with beginning their journey.

Item 8.
- A. Thereby their inability to finance themselves caused many disputes and disagreements,
- B. Although their inability to finance themselves caused many disputes and disagreements,
- C. Nevertheless their inability to finance themselves caused many disputes and disagreements,

- D. Despite their inability to finance themselves caused many disputes and disagreements,
- E. In spite of their inability to finance themselves caused many disputes and disagreements,

Item 9.
- A. the Pilgrims finally managing to obtain financing
- B. the Pilgrims finally managed obtaining financing
- C. the Pilgrims finally were managed obtaining financing
- D. the Pilgrims finally were managed to obtain financing
- E. the Pilgrims finally managed to obtain financing

Item 10.
- A. from a well-known and considerable London businessman named Thomas Weston.
- B. From a well-known and affluent London businessman named Thomas Weston.
- C. from a well-known and unfortunate London businessman named Thomas Weston.
- D. from a well-known and adamant London businessman named Thomas Weston.
- E. from a well-known and insistent London businessman named Thomas Weston.

Item 11.
- A. Having secured Weston's monetary support, the group returned to England to pick up some additional passengers,
- B. To have secured Weston's monetary support, the group returned to England to pick up some additional passengers,
- C. They have secured Weston's monetary support, the group returned to England to pick up some additional passengers,
- D. When they have secured Weston's monetary support, the group returned to England to pick up some additional passengers,
- E. Having secured Weston's monetary support, the group returned to England to pick up some additional passengers

Item 12.
- A. and it boarded a large ship called the Mayflower on September 16, 1620.
- B. and he or she boarded a large ship called the Mayflower on September 16, 1620.
- C. and one boarded a large ship called the Mayflower on September 16, 1620.

D. and they boarded a large ship called the Mayflower on September 16, 1620.
E. and those boarded a large ship called the Mayflower on September 16, 1620.

Item 13.
A. After 65 days at sea, the pilgrim's reached America.
B. After 65 days at sea, the Pilgrims' reached America.
C. After 65 days at sea, the Pilgrims reached America.
D. After 65 days at sea, Pilgrim's reached America.
E. After 65 days at sea, Pilgrims' reached America.

Item 14.
A. Plymouth a town about 35 miles southeast of Boston in the New England state of Massachusetts
B. Plymouth, a town about 35 miles southeast of Boston in the New England state of Massachusetts,
C. Plymouth, a town about 35 miles southeast of Boston in the New England, state of Massachusetts
D. Plymouth, a town about 35 miles southeast of Boston in the New England, state of Massachusetts,
E. Plymouth, a town about 35 miles southeast of Boston, in the New England, state of Massachusetts,

Item 15.
A. was established by the Pilgrims in December 21, 1620.
B. was established by the Pilgrims on December 21, 1620.
C. was established by the Pilgrims at December 21, 1620.
D. was established by the Pilgrims upon December 21, 1620.
E. was established by the Pilgrims during December 21, 1620.

Item 16.
A. Even though the early days of this new lives were filled with hope and promise,
B. Even though the early days of that new lives were filled with hope and promise,
C. Even though the early days of their new lives were filled with hope and promise,
D. Even though the early days of these new live were filled with hope and promise,
E. Even though the early days of those new live were filled with hope and promise,

Item 17.
- A. the harsh winter proved being too much for some of the settlers.
- B. the harsh winter proved to be too much for some of the settlers.
- C. the harsh winter proved to being too much for some of the settlers.
- D. the harsh winter proved been too much for some of the settlers.
- E. the harsh winter proved to been too much for some of the settlers.

Item 18.
- A. Near half of the Pilgrims died during that first winter,
- B. Nearly half of the Pilgrims died during that first winter,
- C. Nearly of half of the Pilgrims died during that first winter,
- D. Near of half of the Pilgrims died during that first winter,
- E. Almost near half of the Pilgrims died during that first winter,

Item 19.
- A. but those who lived go on to work hard and prosper.
- B. but those who lived goes on to work hard and prosper.
- C. but those who lived going on to work hard and prosper.
- D. but those who lived went on to work hard and prosper.
- E. but those who lived had went on to work hard and prosper.

Item 20.

If the student removed the last sentence of the essay, how would this affect the essay?
- A. The essay would have more emphasis on the hardships of the Pilgrims.
- B. The comments on the early days of the Pilgrims would have increased importance.
- C. The historical account of the Pilgrims would lack continuity.
- D. The essay would lack a sense of focus.
- E. The essay would lack a proper conclusion.

Essay 4 – Brain Wave Research

[1] In 1929 that electrical activity in the human brain was first discovered. [2] Hans Berger, the German psychiatrist made the discovery, [3] was despondent to find out, in contrast to, that his research was quickly dismissed by many other scientists.

[4] The work of Berger was confirmed three years later, in 1932, when Edgar Adrian a Briton, [5] clearly demonstrated that the brain, like the heart, is profuse in its electrical activity.
[6] Because of Adrian's work, it know that the electrical impulses [7] in the brain called brain waves are a mixture of four different frequencies, [8] that are based on the number of electrical impulses [9] that occurring in the brain per second.

[10] Accordingly, there are four types of brain waves as follows, alpha, beta, delta, and theta.
[11] Alpha waves occur in a state of relaxation, while beta waves occur when a person is alert.
[12] In addition, delta waves take place for sleep, but they can also occur dysfunctionally when the brain has been severely damaged. [13] Finally, theta waves are a frequency of [14] somewhere in between alpha and delta. [15] Seems that the purpose of theta waves is solely to facilitate the combination of the other brain waves.

[16] The whole notion of brain waves feeds into the current controversy about brain death.
[17] Some believe that brain death is characterized by the failure of the cerebral cortex to function. [18] On the other hand, anothers say that mere damage to the cerebral cortex is not enough. [19] They assert that brain stem function must also cease before can a person be declared dead because the cerebral cortex is responsible for other bodily processes.

Item 1.
- A. In 1929 that electrical activity in the human brain was first discovered.
- B. It in 1929 that electrical activity in the human brain was first discovered.
- C. It was in 1929 that electrical activity in the human brain was first discovered.
- D. It in 1929 was that electrical activity in the human brain was first discovered.
- E. That in 1929 electrical activity in the human brain was first discovered.

Item 2.
- A. Hans Berger, the German psychiatrist made the discovery,
- B. Hans Berger, the German psychiatrist had made the discovery,
- C. Hans Berger, the German psychiatrist who made the discovery,
- D. Hans Berger, the German psychiatrist whom made the discovery,
- E. Hans Berger, the German psychiatrist which made the discovery,

Item 3.
- A. was despondent to find out, in contrast to, that his research was quickly dismissed by many other scientists.
- B. was despondent to find out, likewise, that his research was quickly dismissed by many other scientists.
- C. was despondent to find out, but, that his research was quickly dismissed by many other scientists.
- D. was despondent to find out, though, that his research was quickly dismissed by many other scientists.
- E. was despondent to find out, although, that his research was quickly dismissed by many other scientists.

Item 4.
- A. The work of Berger was confirmed three years later, in 1932, when Edgar Adrian a Briton,
- B. The work of Berger was confirmed three years later, in 1932, when Edgar Adrian, a Briton,
- C. The work of Berger was confirmed three years later, in 1932, when Edgar Adrian a Briton

- D. The work of Berger was confirmed three years later, in 1932, when Edgar Adrian a Briton;
- E. The work of Berger was confirmed three years later, in 1932, when Edgar Adrian, a Briton;

Item 5.
- A. clearly demonstrated that the brain, like the heart, is profuse in its electrical activity.
- B. demonstrated that the clearly brain, like the heart, is profuse in its electrical activity.
- C. demonstrated that the brain, like clearly the heart, is profuse in its electrical activity.
- D. demonstrated that the brain, like the heart clearly, is profuse in its electrical activity.
- E. demonstrated that the brain, like the heart, is profuse clearly in its electrical activity.

Item 6.
- A. Because of Adrian's work, it know that the electrical impulses
- B. Because of Adrian's work, it known that the electrical impulses
- C. Because of Adrian's work, it is known that the electrical impulses
- D. Because of Adrian's work, we known that the electrical impulses
- E. Because of Adrian's work, one known that the electrical impulses

Item 7.
- A. in the brain called brain waves are a mixture of four different frequencies,
- B. in the brain, called brain waves are a mixture of four different frequencies,
- C. in the brain called brain waves, are a mixture of four different frequencies,
- D. in the brain, called brain waves, are a mixture of four different frequencies,
- E. in the brain, called brain waves, are a mixture, of four different frequencies,

Item 8.
- A. that are based on the number of electrical impulses
- B. that based on the number of electrical impulses
- C. which are based on the number of electrical impulses
- D. which based on the number of electrical impulses
- E. are based on the number of electrical impulses

Item 9.
- A. that occurring in the brain per second.
- B. that occurred in the brain per second.
- C. that had occurred in the brain per second.
- D. that have occurrence in the brain per second.
- E. that occur in the brain per second.

Item 10.
- A. Accordingly, there are four types of brain waves as follows, alpha, beta, delta, and theta.
- B. Accordingly, there are four types of brain waves as follows: alpha, beta, delta, and theta.
- C. Accordingly, there are four types of brain waves as follows; alpha, beta, delta, and theta.
- D. Accordingly, there are four types of brain waves as follows alpha, beta, delta, and theta.
- E. Accordingly, there are four types of brain waves as follows. Alpha, beta, delta, and theta.

Item 11.
- A. Alpha waves occur in a state of relaxation, while beta waves occur when a person is alert.
- B. Alpha waves occur in a state of relaxation, rather beta waves occur when a person is alert.
- C. Alpha waves occur in a state of relaxation, rather than beta waves occur when a person is alert.
- D. Alpha waves occur in a state of relaxation, instead of waves occur when a person is alert.
- E. Alpha waves occur in a state of relaxation, as for beta waves occur when a person is alert.

Item 12.
- A. In addition, delta waves take place for sleep, but they can also occur dysfunctionally when the brain has been severely damaged.
- B. In addition, delta waves take place during sleep, but they can also occur dysfunctionally when the brain has been severely damaged.
- C. In addition, delta waves take place since sleep, but they can also occur dysfunctionally when the brain has been severely damaged.
- D. In addition, delta waves take place with sleep, but they can also occur dysfunctionally when the brain has been severely damaged.
- E. In addition, delta waves take place at sleep, but they can also occur dysfunctionally when the brain has been severely damaged.

Item 13.
- A. Finally, theta waves are a frequency of
- B. Finally, theta waves are of a frequency
- C. Finally, theta waves of are a frequency
- D. Finally, of theta waves are a frequency
- E. Finally, theta waves are a of frequency

Item 14.
- A. somewhere in between alpha and delta.
- B. somewhere with between alpha and delta.
- C. somewhere in besides alpha and delta.
- D. somewhere at between alpha and delta.
- E. somewhere at besides alpha and delta.

Item 15.
- A. Seems that the purpose of theta waves is solely to facilitate the combination of the other brain waves.
- B. Seemingly that the purpose of theta waves is solely to facilitate the combination of the other brain waves.
- C. It seemingly that the purpose of theta waves is solely to facilitate the combination of the other brain waves.

- D. It is seemingly that the purpose of theta waves is solely to facilitate the combination of the other brain waves.
- E. It seems that the purpose of theta waves is solely to facilitate the combination of the other brain waves.

Item 16.
- A. The whole notion of brain waves feeds into the current controversy about brain death.
- B. The whole notion of brain waves feeds at the current controversy about brain death.
- C. The whole notion of brain waves feeds with the current controversy about brain death.
- D. The whole notion of brain waves feeds against the current controversy about brain death.
- E. The whole notion of brain waves feeds for the current controversy about brain death.

Item 17.
- A. Some believe that brain death is characterized by the failure of the cerebral cortex to function.
- B. Some people's belief that brain death is characterized by the failure of the cerebral cortex to function.
- C. Some peoples' belief that brain death is characterized by the failure of the cerebral cortex to function.
- D. Certain peoples believe that brain death is characterized by the failure of the cerebral cortex to function.
- E. Certain believe that brain death is characterized by the failure of the cerebral cortex to function.

Item 18.
- A. On the other hand, anothers say that mere damage to the cerebral cortex is not enough.
- B. On the other hand, another say that mere damage to the cerebral cortex is not enough.
- C. On the other hand, others say that mere damage to the cerebral cortex is not enough.

- D. On the other hand, other say that mere damage to the cerebral cortex is not enough.
- E. On the other hand, other's say that mere damage to the cerebral cortex is not enough.

Item 19.
- A. They assert that brain stem function must also cease before can a person be declared dead because the cerebral cortex is responsible for other bodily processes.
- B. They assert that brain stem function must also cease before a person can be declared dead because the cerebral cortex is responsible for other bodily processes.
- C. They assert that brain stem function must also cease before may a person be declared dead because the cerebral cortex is responsible for other bodily processes.
- D. They assert that brain stem function must also cease before might a person can be declared dead because the cerebral cortex is responsible for other bodily processes.
- E. They assert that brain stem function must also cease before a person declared dead because the cerebral cortex is responsible for other bodily processes.

Item 20.

Imagine that the student would like to add the following sentence to the essay. What is the best location for this sentence?

Therefore, for these myriad reasons, it has become very important to measure brain activity.

- A. At the end of the first paragraph.
- B. At the end of the second paragraph.
- C. At the end of the third paragraph.
- D. At the beginning of the last paragraph.
- E. At the end of the last paragraph.

Essay 5 – Cancer Risk

[1] Cancer, a group of mainly than 100 different types of disease, [2] occurs where cells in the body begin to divide abnormally and continue dividing and forming more cells without control or order. [3] All internal organs of the body consist of cells, which normally divide to produce more cells when the body requires them. [4] This is a natural, orderly process, that keeps human beings healthy.

[5] If a cell divides when is not necessary, a large growth called a tumor can form. [6] These tumors can usually be removed, and in many cases, they do not recurrence. [7] Unfortunately, in some cases the cancer at the original tumor spreads. [8] The spread of cancer in such way is called metastasis.

[9] There are some factors which are being known to increase the risk of cancer. [10] Smoking is the single cause largest of death from cancer in the United States. [11] One-third of the death's from cancer each year are related to smoking, [12] making tobacco use the most preventable cause of death in this country.

[13] Choice of food can also be link to cancer. [14] Research shows that there are a link between high-fat food and certain cancers, and being seriously overweight is also a cancer risk. [15] Cancer risk can be reduced with a cut down on fatty food and eating generous amounts of fruit and vegetables.

Item 1.
- A. Cancer, a group of mainly than 100 different types of disease,
- B. Cancer, a group of more than 100 different types of disease,
- C. Cancer, a group of 100 more different types of disease,
- D. Cancer, a group of mostly than 100 different types of disease,
- E. Cancer, a group of almost than 100 different types of disease,

Item 2.
- A. occurs where cells in the body begin to divide abnormally and continue dividing and forming more cells without control or order.
- B. occurs which cells in the body begin to divide abnormally and continue dividing and forming more cells without control or order.
- C. occurs in which cells in the body begin to divide abnormally and continue dividing and forming more cells without control or order.
- D. occurs when cells in the body begin to divide abnormally and continue dividing and forming more cells without control or order.
- E. occurs once when cells in the body begin to divide abnormally and continue dividing and forming more cells without control or order.

Item 3.
- A. All internal organs of the body consist of cells, which normally divide to produce more cells when the body requires them.
- B. All internal organs of the body consist of cells, which divide to normally produce more cells when the body requires them.
- C. All internal organs of the body consist of cells, which divide to produce more normally cells when the body requires them.
- D. All internal organs of the body consist of cells, which divide to produce more cells when normally the body requires them.
- E. All internal organs of the body consist of cells, which divide to produce more cells when the body requires them normally.

Item 4.
- A. This is a natural, orderly process, that keeps human beings healthy.
- B. This is a natural, orderly process that keeps human beings healthy.
- C. This is a natural orderly process, that keeps human beings healthy.
- D. This is a natural orderly process that keeps human beings healthy.
- E. This is a natural orderly, process that keeps human beings healthy.

Item 5.
- A. If a cell divides when is not necessary, a large growth called a tumor can form.
- B. If a cell divides when they are not necessary, a large growth called a tumor can form.
- C. If a cell divides when it is not necessary, a large growth called a tumor can form.
- D. If a cell divides when are not necessary, a large growth called a tumor can form.
- E. If a cell divides when that not necessary, a large growth called a tumor can form.

Item 6.
- A. These tumors can usually be removed, and in many cases, they do not recurrence.
- B. These tumors can usually be removed, and in many cases, they do not make recurrence.
- C. These tumors can usually be removed, and in many cases, they do not recurring.
- D. These tumors can usually be removed, and in many cases, they do not are recurred.
- E. These tumors can usually be removed, and in many cases, they do not recur.

Item 7.
- A. Unfortunately, in some cases the cancer at the original tumor spreads.
- B. Unfortunately, in some cases the cancer from the original tumor spreads.
- C. Unfortunately, in some cases the cancer with the original tumor spreads.
- D. Unfortunately, in some cases the cancer for the original tumor spreads.
- E. Unfortunately, in some cases the cancer below the original tumor spreads.

Item 8.
- A. The spread of cancer in such way is called metastasis.
- B. The spread of cancer in such a way is called metastasis.
- C. The spread of cancer in such ways is called metastasis.
- D. The spread of cancer in such like way is called metastasis.
- E. The spread of cancer in such like ways is called metastasis.

Item 9.
- A. There are some factors which are being known to increase the risk of cancer.
- B. There are some factors which are know to increase the risk of cancer.
- C. There are some factors which are knowing to increase the risk of cancer.
- D. There are some factors which are known to increase the risk of cancer.
- E. There are some factors which have known to increase the risk of cancer.

Item.10
- A. Smoking is the single cause largest of death from cancer in the United States.
- B. Smoking is the single cause of largest death from cancer in the United States.
- C. Smoking is the single cause of death largest from cancer in the United States.
- D. Smoking is the single cause of death from cancer largest in the United States.
- E. Smoking is the largest single cause of death from cancer in the United States.

Item 11.
- A. One-third of the death's from cancer each year are related to smoking,
- B. One-third of the deaths' from cancer each year are related to smoking,
- C. One-third of the deaths from cancer each year are related to smoking,
- D. One-third of cancer's deaths each year are related to smoking,
- E. One-third of cancers' deaths each year are related to smoking,

Item 12.
- A. making tobacco use the most preventable cause of death in this country.
- B. which making tobacco use the most preventable cause of death in this country.
- C. made tobacco use the most preventable cause of death in this country.
- D. which will be making tobacco use the most preventable cause of death in this country.
- E. in making tobacco use the most preventable cause of death in this country.

Item 13.
- A. Choice of food can also be link to cancer.
- B. Choice of food can also be linking to cancer.
- C. Choice of food can also be linked to cancer.
- D. Choice of food can also been linked to cancer.
- E. Choice of food can also link to cancer.

Item 14.
- A. Research shows that there are a link between high-fat food and certain cancers, and being seriously overweight is also a cancer risk.
- B. Research shows that there is a link between high-fat food and certain cancers, and being seriously overweight is also a cancer risk.

    C.   Research shows that there's links between high-fat food and certain cancers, and being seriously overweight is also a cancer risk.

    D.   Research shows that there is existing a link between high-fat food and certain cancers, and being seriously overweight is also a cancer risk.

    E.   Research shows that there in existence a link between high-fat food and certain cancers, and being seriously overweight is also a cancer risk.

Item 15.

    A.   Cancer risk can be reduced with a cut down on fatty food and eating generous amounts of fruit and vegetables.

    B.   Cancer risk can be reduced with cutting down on fatty food and eating generous amounts of fruit and vegetables.

    C.   Cancer risk can be reduced with cutting down fatty food and eating generous amounts of fruit and vegetables.

    D.   Cancer risk can be reduced by cutting down on fatty food and eating generous amounts of fruit and vegetables.

    E.   Cancer risk can be reduced by cut down on fatty food and eating generous amounts of fruit and vegetables.

Item 16.

Suppose the student wants to include an admonition to the reader about how he or she can prevent cancer risks. Which sentence, if added to the end of the essay, would achieve this purpose?

    A.   Accordingly, the government needs to act now to help improve the health of the country.

    B.   Militating against the causes of cancer is a difficult but necessary task.

    C.   It is therefore the responsibility of each individual to try to mitigate cancer risk by living a healthy lifestyle.

    D.   However, these deaths could easily have been avoided.

    E.   Nevertheless, most people agree that trying to prevent cancer risk is extremely important.

ANSWERS TO THE BONUS EXERCISES

Antarctica Essay

1) A

2) C

3) D

4) C

5) A

6) B

7) B

8) B

9) D

10) C

11) A

12) B

13) C

14) B

15) B

16) E

17) C

18) B

19) D

20) E

Population Age-Sex Structure Essay

1) D
2) B
3) A
4) E
5) B
6) C
7) D
8) B
9) C
10) B
11) C
12) B
13) D
14) C
15) E
16) D
17) C
18) B
19) A
20) D
21) E

The Pilgrims Essay

1) C
2) D
3) D
4) D
5) C
6) E
7) C
8) B
9) E
10) B
11) A
12) D
13) C
14) B
15) B
16) C
17) B
18) B
19) D
20) E

Brain Wave Research Essay

1) C
2) C
3) D
4) B
5) A
6) C
7) D
8) C
9) E
10) B
11) A
12) B
13) B
14) A
15) E
16) A
17) A
18) C
19) B
20) E

Cancer Risk Essay

1) B

2) D

3) A

4) B

5) C

6) E

7) B

8) B

9) D

10) E

11) C

12) A

13) C

14) B

15) D

16) C

www.ingramcontent.com/pod-product-compliance
Lightning Source LLC
Chambersburg PA
CBHW081751100526
44592CB00015B/2382